Contents

Author's note

For various reasons I have used different editions and translations of Marx's works for different quotations. All sources are stated in brackets in the text, and publication details are listed in the Bibliography. For biographical information I have relied mainly on David McLellan's *Karl Marx*, though I have also used the biographies by Franz Mehring and Francis Wheen, Alex Callinicos's *The Revolutionary Ideas of Karl Marx*, and the reminiscences of Marx by his son-in-law Paul Lafargue and his disciple Wilhelm Liebknecht.

I would like to dedicate the book to my students in the courses on Marx and Engels and on Marxist thought, whose questions have helped to stimulate some of the arguments in this book.

Marx

Marx

Andrew Collier

ONEWORLD PHILOSOPHERS

ONEWORLD

OXFORD

MARX

Oneworld Publications
(Sales and Editorial)
185 Banbury Road
Oxford OX2 7AR
England
www.oneworld-publications.com

ISBN 1–85168–346–1

Cover design by the Bridgewater Book Company
Typeset by Jayvee, Trivandrum, India
Printed and bound in India by Thomson Press Ltd.

Prologue

Towards the end of his life, Marx wrote the following words in the opening to the programme of the French Workers' Party:

> Considering,
>   That the emancipation of the class of producers involves all mankind, without distinction of sex or race;
>   That the producers can only be free when they are in possession of the means of production;
>   That there are only two forms in which the means of production can belong to them:
>   1. The individual form, which was never a universal phenomenon and is being ever more superseded by the progress of industry,
>   2. The collective form, the material and mental elements for which are created by the very development of capitalist society. (*The First International and After*, p. 376)

The introduction goes on to state the need for a workers' party to use universal manhood suffrage (which had recently been established in France) to secure common ownership of the means of production. There follows a 'minimum programme' of demands for democratic liberties, the eight-hour working day, equal pay for women, and so on.

The statement of the conditions for workers' freedom sums up Marx's political commitment very well. It can be expressed in two words: workers' democracy. Marx is best known as the greatest thinker and writer in the working-class political movements of the nineteenth century, but these movements should be seen in a wider context: as part of the movement for democracy, which grew throughout that century, and bore fruit in the twentieth century in widespread parliamentary democracy, and occasional experiments in more radical forms of democracy. Marx himself was committed to democracy before he became committed to working-class political movements; in all his struggles within those movements his politics was more democratic than that of his opponents – the utopians, the conspiratorial revolutionism of Blanqui, the anarchists, the Lassallean trend in German social democracy.

It has become commonplace since 1917 to contrast democratic with revolutionary socialism. This contrast – misleading even today – would have made no sense in the nineteenth century. Until relatively late in Marx's life, manhood suffrage existed only in some American states (not all – slaves could not vote, and some non-slave-owning states had a property qualification for voting). It existed also briefly in France from the revolution of 1848 to May 1850. Nowhere could women vote. The first fully sovereign state with genuinely universal suffrage (women as well as men) was Australia in 1901, eighteen years after Marx's death. When T.H. Green, the great liberal political philosopher, went to Oxford as a student in the 1850s, he was asked to join the rifle club on the grounds that there might be a repetition of Chartism (a mass movement for democracy) – and presumably students would be expected to go out and shoot democrats. To his credit he replied that he would join and, in that eventuality, desert to the side of the people. In 1848, Marx could sum up the immediate aim of his projected revolution as winning the battle of democracy, which he saw as equivalent to raising the proletariat to the position of ruling class. To be a democrat, in Marx's time, *was* to be a revolutionary.

Marx's espousal of democracy is all the more striking in that it is unique among first-rank German thinkers. Leibniz lived before democracy was on the agenda; Kant and Hegel were advocates of constitutional government, but not universal suffrage; Schopenhauer and Nietzsche were frankly anti-democratic; and in more recent times, Frege wanted to disfranchise Jews, Husserl showed no interest in politics, and Heidegger flirted with the Nazis. Which leaves Marx as the sole democrat among the great German minds.

But what distinguished Marx from most other democrats was his belief that political emancipation was not enough without economic emancipation. The above quote makes it clear that, for the workers, emancipation means democracy in the workplace, not just in the state. Today, when the global market has stripped national parliaments of their economic power, this argument is more relevant than ever.

At two periods of his life, Marx played an active role in organizing working-class and democratic political movements: in the unsuccessful democratic revolution in Germany from 1848, and in the International Working Men's Association (the First International) from 1864. During the rest of his life, his contribution to these movements was through research and writing. In what follows, after a brief account of his life and character, I shall be introducing his thoughts about politics, economics, and social and historical science. I shall not, except in passing, discuss his critique of Hegel's philosophy or his opinions about religion or the arts. The second chapter discusses his most celebrated youthful writing, the *Economic and Philosophical Manuscripts*, written in 1844 at the age of twenty-six, and not published until nearly fifty years after his death. This is in many ways distinct from his later writing, though the degree of continuity and break between the young and the mature Marx is an issue hotly contested by scholars. Later chapters will be by theme rather than by period of his life. In the last two chapters, I shall discuss issues that have arisen out of his work after his death, and his relevance to twenty-first-century concerns.

The main events of Marx's life

5 May 1818	Born at Trier, Germany
1830	Entered Frederick William High School, Trier
October 1835	Entered Bonn University to study law

Summer 1836	Engaged to Jenny von Westphalen
October 1836	Transferred to Berlin University
May 1838	Death of his father, Heinrich (Hirschel)
April 1841	Obtained Doctorate in Philosophy
March 1842	Death of Baron von Westphalen (father of Jenny)
October 1842	Becomes editor of the liberal journal *Rheinische Zeitung*
March 1843	*Rheinische Zeitung* suppressed
June 1843	Marriage to Jenny von Westphalen
October 1843	Moved to Paris, where he first encountered socialist and working-class movements, and became a socialist
May 1844	Birth of first daughter Jenny
Summer 1844	Wrote *Economic and Philosophical Manuscripts*
February 1845	Expelled from Paris – moved to Brussels
1845	Wrote *Theses on Feuerbach* and *The German Ideology* (with Engels, who became his lifelong friend at this time)
September 1845	Birth of daughter Laura
December 1846	Birth of first son Edgar
January 1847	Joined Communist League
1848	'Year of Revolutions'
February 1848	*The Communist Manifesto* published
February 1848	French monarchy overthrown
March 1848	Moved to Paris
June 1848	Moved to Cologne. Editor of democratic journal *Neue Rheinische Zeitung*

May 1849	Suppression of *Neue Rheinische Zeitung*. Expulsion from Cologne. Moves to Paris (May) and London (August)
November 1849	Birth of son Guido
September 1950	Death of Guido
December 1850	Settled in Dean Street, Soho, London
March 1851	Birth of daughter Franziska
June 1851	Birth of Frederick, to Helene Demuth (possibly Marx's son)
April 1852	Death of Franziska
November 1852	Communist League dissolved
January 1855	Birth of daughter Eleanor (Tussy)
April 1855	Death of son Edgar
July 1856	Death of Baroness von Westphalen
September 1856	Moved to Grafton Terrace, near Hampstead Heath
November 1863	Death of Marx's mother, Henrietta (née Pressburg)
April 1864	Moved to Modena Villas
September 1864	First International founded
Summer 1865	Lectures which became *Value, Price and Profit* given
September 1867	*Capital* published
April 1868	Marriage of daughter Laura to French socialist Paul Lafargue
1870	Engels moved from Manchester to London
March–May 1871	Paris Commune

October 1872	Marriage of daughter Jenny to French Communard Charles Longuet
May 1875	Wrote *Critique of the Gotha Programme*
1875	Moved to smaller house in Maitland Park Road
May 1880	Wrote *Introduction to Programme of French Workers' Party*
December 1881	Death of Jenny Marx (née von Westphalen)
January 1883	Death of Jenny Longuet (née Marx)
14 March 1883	Death of Karl Marx

Chapter One

The Life of Marx

Karl Marx was born on 5 May 1818 in the small German town of Trier, near the Luxembourg border. Trier is the oldest town in Germany, and in 334 or thereabouts had been the birthplace of another man who changed European history, St Ambrose. The town was part of the Rhineland, had been ruled by Napoleon, and in some ways had benefited by his rule. Though incorporated into Prussia in 1815, it was rather more liberal than most Prussian lands. Karl's father, Heinrich Marx, was a lawyer, and an admirer of Rousseau and the French Enlightenment. His mother, Henrietta, of whom we know rather little, was Dutch. Both parents were Jewish, and there were many rabbis in Karl Marx's ancestry, on both sides of the family. However, Heinrich (whose name had been Hirschel) had converted to Protestantism shortly before Karl's birth, though Karl was not baptised until he was six. The conversion was a matter of convenience rather than conviction and, like most people with a background in such conversions, Karl Marx was never deeply affected by religion. In his school essays he expressed a conventional, rationalistic Protestantism, but as an adult was a lifelong atheist.

Marx was educated in the Frederick William High School in Trier, and went to university at Bonn and later Berlin, initially to study law, though he later moved over to philosophy. Having been brought up by his father on

Enlightenment writers, and introduced by Baron von Westphalen, the father of his future wife, to the romantics, at university he encountered Hegel, whose philosophical system dominated German universities at that time. In Hegel's thought, many apparent opposites are reconciled, for instance the French Revolutionary belief in the sovereignty of reason and the romantics' belief in organic community. Hegel's political philosophy is not a compromise between reason and organic community. It is, in intention, rationalist through and through, and organic through and through. The same could be said, in a different way, of the society Marx was to aim for.

There is a long-standing academic debate on how much Hegel's philosophy influenced that of the mature Marx, which debate I shall avoid introducing into this book wherever possible. But I think Hegel's influence on Marx's *cultural attitudes* is profound, and left Marx with a far broader outlook and more balanced judgement in these matters than most revolutionaries. I think it would be true to say that what is best in Marx is what is original to him, what is second best is derived from Hegel, and what is mistaken is derived from the Jacobin tradition inherited from the French Revolution.

After obtaining a PhD on the rather obscure topic of the relation between the ancient Greek atomist philosophers Democritus and Epicurus, Marx might have entered an academic career, but his opinions, while not yet socialist, were already democratic and anticlerical, and this was well enough known to make academic employment unlikely. He began to work for a Cologne-based liberal journal, the *Rheinische Zeitung*, of which he soon became editor. This was his first engagement in serious politics. It lasted only a few months, since the journal was suppressed by the censors at the request of the Russian tsar, whom it had attacked. Marx decided to move to Paris to work with Arnold Ruge on a projected new journal, the *Deutsche–Französische Jahrbucher*. While working for the *Rheinische Zeitung* one experience influenced Marx deeply. He had to consider the issue of 'thefts of wood' by the peasants of the Moselle wine-growing area – thefts according to the property owners, the exercise of their traditional right of gathering wood according to the peasants. This alerted Marx to the roots of politics in the social and economic conditions of the people.

Before leaving Germany, Marx married Jenny von Westphalen, to whom he had been engaged for seven years. They were married in Kreuznach, and stayed there for the summer of 1843, until everything was ready for them to go to Paris. In Paris, their first child, also called Jenny, was born. She nearly died of convulsions there, and was saved by the presence of mind of the poet Heinrich Heine, one of the few friends with whom Marx never quarrelled.

In Paris too, Marx encountered for the first time not only socialist writers, but the urban wage-earning class, the proletariat. He also began to study and criticize the Scottish and English economists, Adam Smith and David Ricardo. From this period dates Marx's conversion to socialism, marked by his writing the *Economic and Philosophical Manuscripts*, which start with criticism of these economists and continue to make a case against the dehumanization of people under capitalism. This I shall discuss in the next chapter.

While in Paris, Marx had his first prolonged meeting with Frederick Engels, who was to be his lifelong friend and co-worker. Engels, while his own judgement that 'Marx was a genius, the rest of us merely talented' was no doubt true, had a much more practical knowledge of capitalism. His father was a textile manufacturer with a factory in Manchester as well as one in Wuppertal, and Engels had spent some time in England – the only significant country where the proletariat was a majority. Engels's first book was *The Condition of the Working Class in England*, as empirical and practical as Marx's early writings were speculative and theoretical. During their common exile after the defeat of the German revolution, Engels worked as a manager in his father's factory, which enabled him to help out the Marx family financially. It has become customary in many circles to blame everything wrong about later Marxism on Engels, but this is wholly unfair. He was as committed to democracy and to an open approach to science as was Marx, and rather more aware than Marx of environmental issues and the oppression of women.

Early in 1845, there occurred the first of a series of expulsions of Marx from countries where he lived. He had been contributing to a journal called *Vorwärts* which acted as a forum for German radicals in Paris. The journal was closed by the French minister of the interior, and writers Marx, Arnold Ruge and Heinrich Heine were expelled from France. Marx moved to Belgium where his family lived for the next three years in Brussels. Here they were joined by Helene Demuth, a family servant of the von Westphalens, who then stayed with the Marxes for the rest of their lives, following them into exile in England. It was in Brussels that Marx's second daughter, Laura, was born, followed by his first son, Edgar, a year later.

Several other socialist friends and acquaintances moved to Brussels too, including most importantly Frederick Engels, with whom Marx began to work on their book *The German Ideology*. They could not find a publisher for this book, and eventually abandoned it 'to the gnawing criticism of the mice', as they said (and when it was exhumed and published in the twentieth century, parts had actually been destroyed by mice). The first section of this book, on the German humanist philosopher Feuerbach, who had influenced them profoundly but whom they now found it necessary to go beyond, is a classic statement of their programme for a science of history, and will be discussed later in this book. The later sections of *The German Ideology* are rambling polemics, which have lost much of their interest with the decline of interest in their targets. Marx's other most important work of this period is his brilliant, pithy *Theses on Feuerbach*, which was intended for self-clarification not publication, but which Engels later published. These eleven theses, each only a sentence or a paragraph long, contain some of Marx's most quoted words, such as the much misunderstood eleventh thesis: 'The philosophers have only interpreted the world, in various ways; the point is to change it.'

Apart from writing and studying the economists, Marx became involved with various socialist groups at this time, meeting – and quarrelling with – the German utopian socialist Weitling, and eventually, in 1847, joining the League of the Just, a German group of socialist workers in exile in various countries and in a dozen cities of Germany itself. This league, partly due to the influence of Marx and Engels, reorganized itself in this year, replacing conspiratorial with democratic forms of organization, renaming itself the Communist League, and adopting as its slogan 'Proletarians of all countries – unite' instead of 'All men are brothers'; apparently Marx (despite his admiration for Robert Burns's poetry) said that there were many men whose brother he did not wish to be. They also commissioned Marx and Engels to write a manifesto, which was published early in 1848 as the *Manifesto of the Communist Party* – though the Communist League was not really a party. It is the first statement of Marx's mature political position, and is normally known as *The Communist Manifesto.*

The year of 1848 has gone down in history as the 'Year of Revolutions' and, almost simultaneously with the manifesto's publication, the French monarchy fell, and movements for democracy began in many European countries. In England the Chartist Movement, which had been dormant for a few years, revived with its demands for manhood suffrage, annual parliaments and other democratic reforms. Marx regarded this as the first real working-class party. But in Germany too the demands for a parliamentary constitution and for national unity were made. Marx, wanting to be where the action was, returned first to Paris, and then in June to Cologne, where he became editor of the *Neue Rheinische Zeitung,* a journal whose programme was a unified democratic republic of Germany, and the liberation of Poland from Russia – which would have involved war with Russia. The journal was not run by the Communist League, and had liberal as well as socialist backers. In fact, throughout the German revolution, Marx, though he by no means abandoned his socialist aims, concentrated on what he saw as the next step, the democratic republic, and his main criticism of the bourgeois parties was not that they were not socialist but that they were cowardly and compromising in their pursuit of democracy. Towards the end of the revolutionary period, he saw that the bourgeoisie was too scared to lead a revolution, and he turned to more explicitly communist agitation, but by this time the revolution was in retreat.

The German revolution never got as far as bringing down any monarchies, and even the moves towards parliamentary government were half measures and soon lost. In May 1849, the *Neue Rheinische Zeitung* was suppressed, and Marx was once more subjected to an expulsion order. At first he went again to France, where he acted in some official capacity on behalf of the German democrats. However, the revolution was in retreat in France too, and Marx was expelled from Paris again, sailing for England in August. For the rest of his life, he lived in London, at first in Soho, in considerable hardship – though Marx's income was irregular rather than low by working-class standards, and both generosity and mismanagement contributed to the hardship. In the next six years three Marx children died: two (Guido and Franziska), who were born in London, died as babies; the other, Edgar, died at the age of eight. Marx's daughter Eleanor (always known as Tussy), was born while the Marxes lived in Soho. She was to survive her father and become active in the English labour movement. Also in this Soho period a son, Frederick, was born to Helene Demuth and, according to a document which came to light in 1962, Marx was the father. Frederick was not brought up by the Marxes or by his mother, though he maintained contact with his mother, and became friendly with Marx's daughters later. Frederick also became active in the English labour movement, and was a founder member of Hackney Labour Party. He survived all the others and died in 1929. Engels is said to have accepted paternity to save the Marxes embarrassment. Helene Demuth remained part of the Marx household, and seems to have been as close to Jenny Marx as to Karl in later years. It is quite possible that the document implicating Marx as Frederick's father is a forgery – see Terrell Carver's biography of Engels for the evidence.

In an attempt to get a regular income, at one time Marx applied for a job as a railway clerk, but was turned down because his handwriting was illegible (it was).

At first during his exile, Marx engaged in the unedifying politics of the exiled communists and other German democrats, but soon tired of the sectarianism and, after the dissolution of the Communist League in 1852, took no part in active politics until the foundation of the First International in 1864. During this period, Marx spent a great deal of time in the library of the British Museum, researching for his greatest work, *Capital*. He did not expect his work on economics to take so long, and in 1851 told Engels that, 'In five weeks I will be through with the whole economic shit'; but he left huge boxes of unfinished manuscripts on economics when he died, even though it is reported that his last words were, 'Go away, last words are for those who have not said enough already.' To make a living, he also wrote numerous articles for the *New York Tribune*, some of which were mere pot-boilers, though his enthusiasm for the anti-slavery north in the American Civil War – and for President Lincoln – was completely genuine.

Aside from this source of income, he was always dependent too on Engels's generosity. However, a legacy from Baroness von Westphalen, Jenny's mother, enabled the family to move from their rooms in Soho to a house near Hampstead Heath, where they loved to walk and picnic.

Marx became involved in active politics again when the International Working Men's Association (the First International) was founded in 1864. It was founded not by Marx but by groups of French and English workers who saw the need for international solidarity, partly for the practical reason that employers broke strikes by importing workers from one country to another as blacklegs. The founders were not Marxists: the English were liberal trade unionists, the French mostly followers of the co-operative anarchism of Proudhon. But Marx joined the Association straight away, and became its leading figure, writing the Inaugural Address and Provisional Rules. He retained this position throughout the First International's existence, although Marxists were never more than a minority of its members, partly because Marx had something in common with each of the other factions, and they had little in common with each other. The German socialists, among whom he already had some followers, could not play a full part in the life of the First International due to the laws in Germany. The main threat to his leadership came from Bakunin, a revolutionary Russian anarchist with considerable support in the Mediterranean sections of the International. Bakunin wanted to abolish the state at once, while Marx, as we shall see, thought that a workers' state was necessary until classes had disappeared, when the state would 'wither away'. Bakunin presented himself as a libertarian against Marx's authoritarianism, and opposed centralization in the International. But he was not consistently more libertarian, for on the other hand he wanted to make atheism a condition of membership of the International, which Marx regarded as imposing a dogma (albeit one with which he agreed) on the working class. It would probably have excluded most of the English members. The split between Marx and Bakunin, which may partly have been based on personal suspiciousness on both sides, was one of the reasons why the International was so short-lived (it petered out after Marx got Bakunin expelled and had its centre moved to New York in 1872). But a quarrel between these two was more or less inevitable given Bakunin's addiction to cloak-and-dagger conspiracies, fantasies of powerful organizations which had no existence in reality, and indeed his virulent anti-Semitism.

But one extraordinary event took place during the lifetime of the International, though not at its instigation: the Paris Commune. After the defeat of France in the Franco–Prussian War and the abdication of Napoleon III, the provisional government tried to disarm Paris. The National Guard resisted, taking over the city and holding elections on manhood suffrage. The resultant council of ninety-two members included seventeen members of the International, but the International was in no way in control of it, as the press and governments later claimed. In fact the majority of its members were lower-middle class rather than working class, and harked back to the great French Revolution of 1789, though there were notable minorities of Proudhonian anarchists and Blanquists (the latter were revolutionary workers who, unlike Marx, worked in a conspiratorial manner, and looked for a dictatorship by a revolutionary élite after the Revolution, rather than the broader democratic workers' state proposed by Marx). The measures of the Paris Commune were quite moderate reforms – abolition of nightwork for bakers, a law against reducing wages, and so on. The only socialistic measure was the handing over of enterprises whose bosses had abandoned Paris to the workers to run as co-operatives, under reserve of compensation. The Commune used terror relatively little, and only in response to greater terror on the part of its enemies. Those Communards who were members of the International, though 'extremists' in terms of class politics, were 'moderates' so far as terror was concerned. The worst outrage committed under the Paris Commune was the massacre of fifty hostages, which was not ordered by the Commune, but carried out by a lynch mob in the last days of the Commune when its supporters were being massacred in thousands. The leading First Internationalist in the Paris Commune, Varlin, tried unsuccessfully to rescue the hostages. He himself was brutally murdered by anti-Commune government soldiers soon afterwards. The numbers of Commune supporters executed after its defeat ran into tens of thousands – several times as many as those guillotined in the great French Revolution.

Marx was initially sceptical about the Commune's chances of success – a scepticism that was borne out by the fall of the Commune after just over two months. But he not only defended the Communards' courage and their right to self-defence, but saw it as the first intimation of what a workers' state would be like. This view will be discussed later.

After the fall of the Paris Commune and the decline of the First International, Marx's main political attentions turned to Germany, where there were two working-class political parties, one following Lassalle, and tending to favour German unity even under Prussian domination, the other (the 'Eisenachers'), with more support in south Germany where Prussia was regarded with suspicion, and with more willingness to make alliances with liberal bourgeois parties. Marx supported the Eisenachers, one of whose leaders, Liebknecht, he had known for a long time. In 1875 the two parties merged at a conference in Gotha, and became the German Social Democratic Party (SPD) which, much changed in a rightwards direction, still exists. Marx found a fair bit to object to in the Gotha Programme adopted by the party, which he saw as too Lassallean. Among other things he objected to the statement that all classes but the proletariat were 'one reactionary mass'. Marx wanted to make a distinction between the landed aristocracy who supported Bismarck and the liberal bourgeoisie who should be supported against them, and more particularly the lower-middle class and peasantry who needed to be won over to the workers' side. He suspected – what later turned out to be true – that Lassalle had been willing to make a deal with Bismarck. However, Marx maintained good if sometimes uneasy relations with the SPD leaders and, at the theoretical level, his influence in the party grew and became paramount. At the practical level, the SPD was much more a party of moderate reform than he or its own members realized.

Towards the end of the 1870s, Marx's health, and that of his wife Jenny, was increasingly bad. McLellan writes that, 'By the turn of the decade the topics of sickness and climate pervaded Marx's letters to the virtual exclusion of all else' (*Karl Marx*, p. 430). Jenny had cancer of the liver, and their daughter Jenny Longuet had cancer of the bladder. Marx himself was suffering from chronic bronchitis and an ulcer on the lung. When he became well enough to go into his wife's room, their daughter Eleanor reports, 'They were young again together – she a loving maid and he a loving youth, who were entering life together – and not an old man devastated by illness and a dying old woman who were taking leave of one another for life' (*Selected Works in Two Volumes*, vol. 1, p. 127). But she died on 2 December 1881. When Engels saw Marx after this, he told Eleanor, 'Moor [Marx] is also dead,' and indeed he did not recover his will to live. In January 1883 Jenny Longuet died aged thirty-eight, and two months later Marx himself died, aged sixty-four. He was buried in Highgate Cemetery, London, where he shares his grave with his wife Jenny, Helene Demuth, his grandson Harry Longuet, who died a few days after Marx, aged four, and his daughter Eleanor (Tussy), who died by her own hand in 1898 after her lover deserted her. The large black bust of Marx which now adorns the grave would not have been to his taste, but has become something of a local landmark.

It is natural that anyone with as strong political opinions as Marx would provoke strong and opposite reactions among different people. But people's reactions at a more personal level could be opposite as well, ranging from an American senator who said, 'I have never seen a man whose bearing was so provoking and intolerable,' to his daughter Eleanor who calls him, 'a man brimming over with humour and good humour ... the kindliest, gentlest, most sympathetic of companions' (McLellan, *Karl Marx*, pp. 453–5). Yet a coherent picture does emerge. In political relations he was a hard man to have against you. When attacking an opponent, he loaded his pen with vitriol. But he did not, I think, confuse the emotions appropriate to politics with those appropriate to personal relations, as so many political activists do. He was devoted to his wife and children; despite his alleged affair with Helene Demuth, his love for his wife – and hers for him – was passionate and lifelong, though Marx later advised that a revolutionary ought not to marry and bring a family into such an insecure existence, and indeed Jenny was often at her wits' end during their long exile. He loved playing with his children; a Prussian spy who visited him during the hard years at Dean Street, Soho, reported that, 'As father and husband, Marx, in spite of his wild and restless character, is the gentlest and mildest of men,' and that the only chair with four legs, which he as a visitor was offered, was being used by the children to play at cooking, and, 'if you sit down you risk a pair of trousers'. Later Marx was a good friend to his grown-up daughters. He took the early deaths of three of his children very badly, commenting, when eight-year-old Edgar died, 'Bacon says that really important men have so many relations with nature and the world that they recover easily from every loss. I do not belong to these important men.' (Quoted by Alex Callinicos, *The Revolutionary Ideas of Karl Marx*, p. 26.)

He was a loyal and generous friend once he had given his friendship, but he did not suffer fools gladly, and thought that rather a lot of the people he met were fools. He had a caustic wit, and people feared his criticism, yet according to his daughter Eleanor he could discuss and criticize Heine's unfinished poems with Heine in friendship and good humour, though Heine was in general hypersensitive to criticism. Liebknecht says that, as a teacher, Marx had the rare quality of being stern without being discouraging. His sometimes excessively polemical style was an unfortunate legacy to the socialist movement, yet the socialist advocacy by means of objective reporting and explanatory science in *Capital* is unequalled in the literature of politics and social science. What Lessner said about his speech is also true of his writing: 'He never said a superfluous word; every sentence contained an idea and every idea was an essential link in the chain of his argument.' Despite what is sometimes said about him, he was not a snob – though of course he was from the professional middle class by background and education – and he made friends easily among the proletarian members of the Communist League and the First International.

Outside working hours, he was a great student of world literature. He spoke a number of languages, ancient and modern, and admired Aeschylus, Dante, Cervantes, Shakespeare, Goethe and Burns, all of whom he knew in their original languages. He read Aeschylus every year, and drew inspiration from the story of Prometheus stealing the fire of the gods for the benefit of humankind. His daughters knew several Shakespeare plays by heart, and they would be performed in the house. Among moderns, he particularly admired Balzac. He also kept abreast of scientific developments, and was enough of a 'technological determinist' to believe at one time that the discovery of the electric motor would eventually bring the downfall of capitalism. His interest in applied science extended to the critique of new agricultural practices which were impoverishing the soil – an early example of ecological concern (see John Bellamy Foster in *International Socialism Journal* 96, pp. 71–86, October 2002). Aside from intellectual pursuits, his main recreations seem to have been his walks and picnics on Hampstead Heath. He enjoyed wine and beer, and one visitor reports that he was often drunk; but the quantity and quality of his literary output is proof enough that this was not so often as to interfere with his work.

In the Victorian parlour game of 'Confessions' – the equivalent of what modern magazines call a 'quiz' – he gave as his favourite maxim, *Nihil humani a me alienum puto* (I consider that nothing human is alien to me), and as his favourite motto, *De omnibus dubitandum* (You must have doubts about everything). In these respects, he was a true son of the Enlightenment.

Humanism and Alienation

Marx's *Economic and Philosophical Manuscripts* of 1844 are quite unlike anything else he wrote, even the other early writings criticizing Hegel. His later writings are all on specialized topics – either social science (mainly economics) or political commentary, or in a few cases the methodology of social science. The *Economic and Philosophical Manuscripts* (hereafter EPM) encompass all these topics in some measure, but also a theory of human nature, of the place of human beings in the world, and of ethics. Later Marxists have attributed a general worldview to Marx, and called it 'dialectical materialism' (a phrase Marx himself never used). But there is no explicit worldview in Marx's mature works. In the EPM, though, there is. This is one reason for the immense popularity of these manuscripts since their publication in the 1930s.

Because they were not published until the 1930s, 'classical Marxism' – the Marxism of the Second International from 1889–1914 – could take no account of them. Neither did the world Communist movement, as it emerged in the wake of the Russian Revolution of 1917. By the time they were discovered, Stalin was in power in Russia, and Russian Marxism had become ossified. This ossified Marxism was to some extent imitated by the Communist parties in the West and in Asia. The EPM were not welcomed by the official Communist movement, since they did not fit in with this ossified Marxism. However, they had immense influence outside the bloc, and once Stalin died and free-thought revived inside the Communist bloc, they became widely discussed there too. Indeed they became used as the manifesto of anti-Stalinist Marxism, to the extent that when the French Communist philosopher, Louis Althusser, made some philosophical criticisms of them, he was quite unfairly regarded as trying to revive Stalinism. Many 'neo-Marxists' came to believe that the EPM were the missing ethical and humanistic core of Marxism.

On the other hand, it is clear that the EPM were not intended for publication, but for self-clarification, when Marx had only just abandoned liberalism for socialism. Marx's son-in-law, Paul Lafargue, reports that Marx hated the idea of any of his work being published before he had prepared it for publication, and would rather have seen it burnt. If that wish had been fulfilled, we would have had neither the EPM, nor the later volumes of *Capital*, nor the work known as the *Grundrisse*, which is transitional from the early to the mature work. The EPM do have some weaknesses that Marx would not have tolerated had he intended them for publication. It is not true of them, as it is of his published writings, that there are no wasted sentences. There are a lot of rhetorical flourishes, and some embarrassingly bad arguments. For instance, since as an atheist he rejected the idea of the creation of humankind, and yet since he was writing before Darwin he had no alternative account, he tried by an entirely sophistic argument to show that the question of how we originated was a pseudo-question (*Early Writings*, p. 357).

However, the core of the EPM is the twin ideas of alienated labour, and humanism – the latter being at once a theory of human nature, an ethic, and a methodology of social science. Let us start with alienated labour (I use this translation since it has become standard, though 'estranged labour' is more accurate).

Marx starts from the claim that,

> The externalization of the worker in his product means not only that his labour becomes an object, an *external* existence, but that it exists *outside him*, independently of him and alien to him, and begins to confront him as an autonomous power; that the life which he has bestowed on the object confronts him as hostile and alien. (*Early Writings*, p. 324)

What does this mean? In the first place, that the product does not belong to the worker, it belongs to his employer. But there is more to it than that. The product is seen as having a life of its own, which works *against* the worker. At the simplest level we might think of the case in which by working hard the worker contributes to overproduction, the market is glutted, and the worker thrown out of work. Or the capitalist uses the wealth produced by the worker to buy machinery which makes the worker redundant. But I think there is a more general point here: the 'sorcerer's apprentice' aspect of capitalism. In stories of the sorcerer's apprentice, this unfortunate person has learnt how to conjure up spirits to serve him, but not how to put them to rest. Capitalism conjures up powers which it cannot control. Today with the environmental crisis threatening human existence, this is more relevant than ever. In Marx's own time, the 'crises of overproduction' were the chief example: a kind of 'famine' which would have been regarded as impossible in any pre-capitalist society – a famine in which workers were starving because they had produced too much.

Marx however does not at this point discuss alienation as a feature of the world market, but as a feature of the labour process. The product is alien to the worker, he says, because the activity of production itself is alien to the worker.

> What constitutes the alienation of labour?
>
> Firstly, the fact that labour is *external* to the worker, i.e. does not belong to his essential being; that he therefore does not confirm himself in his work, but denies himself, feels miserable and not happy, does not develop free mental and physical energy, but mortifies his flesh and ruins his mind. Hence the worker feels himself only when he is not working; when he is working he does not feel himself. He is at home when he is not working, and not at home when he is working. His labour is therefore not voluntary but forced, it is *forced labour*. It is therefore not the satisfaction of a need, but a mere *means* to satisfy needs outside itself. Its alien character is clearly demonstrated by the fact that as soon as no physical or other compulsion exists it is shunned like the plague. (*Early Writings*, p. 326)

In part this is the simple point that a worker's time at work is not his or her own, it is 'the boss's time'. Yet in a deeper sense, it is essentially the worker's time: it is a fragment of his or her life, not of the boss's. We have got so used to the idea that time is property that can be sold, alienated, that it does not strike us as strange, but it should. My time is in its essence no more the boss's time because I have sold it to him than my ancestors become your ancestors because I sell you their bones.

But there is more to the problem than this; it is linked to the humanism that I shall describe shortly: the worker's labour is his or her life activity, and ought to be a fulfilment; but it is not, it is an imposition, and is only endured as a means to an external end – the pay cheque.

In these passages the concept of alienation is serving the functions of two concepts used later by Marx. The first is exploitation. Marx makes it quite clear here that the worker's labour and product are alienated because they are appropriated by someone else, the capitalist. The second is *inversion*. The proper relation of producer to product is that the producer dominates the product; under conditions of alienation, this is inverted. This theme of producer/product inversion does not disappear from the later Marx. For instance, in *The Communist Manifesto* he says:

> In bourgeois society, living labour is but a means to increase accumulated labour [i.e. capital]. In communist society, accumulated labour is but a means to enrich, to promote the existence of the labourer.
>
> In bourgeois society, therefore, the past dominates the present; in communist society, the present dominates the past. In bourgeois society capital is independent and has individuality, while the living person is dependent and has no individuality. (*The Revolutions of 1848*, p. 81)

But to understand this concept of inversion as it appears in the EPM we need to look at Marx's view of humankind and our place in nature. It is Marx's view that in order to discern the nature of any animal, one needs to study not just the animal but its products: we study ants by studying ant-hills, beavers by studying dams, and so on. Likewise with humankind:

> It is therefore in his fashioning of the objective that man really proves himself to be a *species-being*. Such production is his active species-life.

Through it nature appears as *his* work and his reality. The object of labour is therefore the *objectification of the species-life of man*: for man reproduces himself not only intellectually, in his consciousness, but actively and actually, and he can therefore contemplate himself in a world he himself has created. (*Early Writings*, p. 329)

(When Marx is writing about 'man' he generally uses the German word 'Mensch', which is not specific to the male sex. I stick with the standard translation, but when paraphrasing Marx I will use the term 'humankind'.) We can see the nature of humankind in the towns and countryside that we have made, and indeed in industry, despite the alienated form it takes at present:

It can be seen how the history of *industry* and the *objective* existence of industry as it has developed is the *open* book of the essential powers of man, man's psychology present in tangible form. (*Early Writings*, p. 354)

Industry is the *real* historical relationship of nature, and hence of natural science, to man. If it is then conceived as the *exoteric* revelation of man's *essential powers*, the *human* essence of nature or the *natural* essence of man can also be understood. (*Early Writings*, p. 355)

It may seem strange that this humanist Jerusalem is 'builded here among those dark satanic mills' (Blake), but of course Marx recognizes that, in *existing* industry, the human essence can only be read in an alienated form; nevertheless even here it can be read, for the transformation of our world through knowledge and productive work reveals the specific capacities of our species. How does this reveal our nature as different from other species? Marx says:

The practical creation of an *objective world*, the *fashioning* of inorganic nature, is proof that man is a conscious species-being, i.e. a being which treats the species as its own essential being or itself as a species-being. It is true that animals also produce. They build nests and dwellings, like the bee, the beaver, the ant, etc. But they produce only their own immediate needs or those of their young; they produce one-sidedly while man produces universally; they produce only when immediate physical need compels them to do so, while man produces even when he is free from physical need, and truly produces only in freedom from such need ... Animals produce only according to the standards and needs of the species to which they belong, while man is capable of producing according to the standards of every species and of applying to each object its inherent standard; hence man also produces in accordance with the laws of beauty. (*Early Writings*, pp. 328–9)

This is not just a matter of us putting foresight into our production, though that is part of it. It is also that, because we produce with tools, with our products, we can produce in *varied* ways, and can *develop* our productive powers. Hence, while animals produce in the same way century after century and remain dependent on their specific evolutionary niches to do so, we have a history as producers, and can adapt to a huge range of habitats by *working on them*. Hence one might say that the evolutionary niche for humankind is a niche for workers. This also means that human evolution is exosomatic, that is, we develop our powers by making things outside our own bodies; we have therefore ceased to evolve by natural selection, since the changes we make to our life conditions make new things advantageous to us faster than 'the survival of the fittest' can select for those that were more advantageous before.

To express the matter this way is a little anachronistic, since Marx was writing before Darwin, but it helps to capture the main points, namely,

1. that human nature is writ large in the environment that we produce
2. that we produce in a cumulative way, not repetitively like other species
3. that since our environment is essential to what we are, in transforming our environment we transform ourselves. To these points can be added
4. that we do not only produce to live, but in some measure for its own sake, or for the sake of beauty.

And from these points Marx derives two conclusions about human nature: firstly, that the core of human nature is productive labour: 'The whole character of a species, its species-character, resides in the nature of its life activity, and free conscious activity constitutes the species-character of man' (*Early Writings*, p. 328); and secondly that the concrete psychology of people differs from epoch to epoch as our natural and social environment is transformed.

Now to return to the question of alienation. According to Marx, it is precisely with respect to our essence, productive labour, that we are alienated. It is in productive activity that we should be most at home, and a few lucky ones – for instance artists – still are. But workers feel least at home in their work, most at home when resting or in the pub.

We are so used to seeing the working part of our lives as a mere means to making money to finance the non-working part of our lives that it seems paradoxical to idealize work in this way. But of course Marx is not saying that we should come to enjoy our alienated labour. One who did that would be doubly alienated. (A common misunderstanding of alienation is that it is a subjective feeling that could be removed by clever personnel management – a pretentious synonym for being fed up. If a worker's time and product are the property of another, he or she is alienated, even if enjoying the job.) Rather, Marx is saying that in a society fit for humans, labour would be very different from what it is now – firstly in that, even if the work was dreary in itself, the workers would know that it was for themselves that they worked; but also in that under such conditions steps would be taken to make work a fitting occupation for an intelligent and creative species. If one wants an image of such a society, William Morris's *News from Nowhere* gives one: boring jobs, when they are really necessary, have been mechanized, and work is either creative craft work or healthy outdoor work – both kinds of work which people do, even now, often choose to do in their spare time. (Morris's utopia is so close to the concerns of the EPM that I wonder whether Engels had the manuscripts in his flat in London, and orally translated passages of them to Morris on some of Morris's visits to his flat.)

The alienation of the human essence – productive labour – creates a totally different moral atmosphere from that, which, if Marx is right, is natural to humankind. It makes people egoistic, not only in the sense that it sets everyone in mutual competition for survival, and thus corrupts our relations with our fellow humans, but also in the sense that it destroys our feel for the intrinsic value of things.

> Private property has made us so stupid and one-sided that an object is only *ours* when we have it, when it exists for us as capital or when we directly possess, eat, drink, wear, inhabit it etc., in short, when we *use* it. (*Early Writings*, p. 351)

> The dealer in minerals sees only the commercial value, and not the beauty and peculiar nature of the minerals; he lacks a mineralogical sense. (p. 353)

Just as work relates us to nature and to the world we create out of it, so our senses need to be educated by the world of things – we need to *acquire* a 'mineralogical sense'. To have such senses which centre on the object, not on our appropriation of it, is for Marx quite natural to us when not suffering from alienation, since nature is our 'inorganic body' (p. 328). As our inorganic body, we both depend on it for life, and need to care for it.

Two things are often said about Marx and human nature: (1) that he doesn't take account of human nature and this vitiates his whole theory; and (2) that he believed that there is no such thing as human nature. Let us look at these in turn.

Those who say that Marx ignores human nature usually mean by 'human nature' egoism, selfishness. Marx does not deny that in existing capitalist society people tend to be narrowly egoistic. Since they must compete and do their neighbours down in order to survive, they have to be. To look at people in capitalist society and conclude that human nature is egoism is like looking at people in a factory where the pollution is destroying their lungs and saying that it is human nature to cough. Marx's view of human nature whereby we change ourselves by changing our environment entails that, to discover how people will behave in any given society, one must look at two things: human nature in general, and the way a given society will affect human nature. As Marx said in criticism of the utilitarian philosopher, Jeremy Bentham:

> To know what is useful for a dog, one must investigate the nature of dogs. This nature is not itself deducible from the principle of utility. Applying this to man, he that would judge all human acts, movements, relations, etc. according to the principle of utility would first have to deal with human nature in general, and then with human

nature as historically modified in each epoch. Bentham does not trouble himself with this. With the driest naiveté he assumes that the modern petty bourgeois, especially the English petty bourgeois, is the normal man. (*Capital*, vol. 1, 1976, pp. 758–9, note 51)

For of course the nature of anything includes not only the properties it always manifests, but its tendency to manifest this property in these circumstances and that in those. It is not the nature of water to be liquid: it is the nature of water to be liquid between zero and one-hundred degrees Celsius. It is not the nature of humans to be egoistic; it is their nature to be egoistic in a society where getting your neighbour's job or undercutting your neighbour's business is necessary to make a living. Outside the market economy, pleasure in productive labour even today involves pleasure in the pleasure given to others. No one would enjoy cooking a meal if they did not expect the eaters to enjoy eating it.

This conception of human nature conflicts with some other conceptions, for instance that of Hobbes, for whom the human desire for power is unlimited, and will always lead to a 'war of all against all' except insofar as people are overawed by a powerful state authority. If Hobbes is right and Marx is wrong, then the advanced form of communism that Marx sometimes refers to, in which distribution is according to need and the state has withered away, would be impossible (though, as we shall see, even a Hobbesian theory of human nature does not rule out some form of socialism). But the fact that people in capitalist societies are much like Hobbes thinks they will be in all societies does not surprise Marx, and is as much evidence for Marx's theory of human nature as for Hobbes's.

This also answers those – often Marxists – who say that Marx did not believe in human nature. They usually mean that he recognizes that people are not the same in all societies. He believed in human nature, but believed that it is part of human nature to behave differently in different kinds of society. (For a detailed disproof of the idea that Marx didn't believe in human nature, see Norman Geras's book *Marx and Human Nature: Refutation of a Legend*.)

While Marx sees capitalist society as unnaturally egoistic, and its economics as essentially amoral (see *Early Writings*, pp. 362–3, where he raises the question whether the sale of people conforms to its laws), he also notes a form of moralism native to capitalism, which reminds one of the worldly asceticism that Weber attributed to Protestants.

> Its true ideal is the *ascetic* but *rapacious* skinflint and the *ascetic* but *productive* slave ... self-denial, the denial of life and of all human needs, is its principal doctrine. The less you eat, drink, buy books, go to the theatre, go dancing, go drinking, think, love, theorize, sing, paint, fence, etc., the more you *save* and the greater will become that treasure which neither moths nor maggots can consume – your *capital*. The less you *are*, the less you give expression to your life, the more you *have*, the greater is your *alienated* life and the more you store up of your estranged life. (p. 361)

Here we can see how the two – conflicting – types of moral philosophy most characteristic of capitalist societies have their foundations in attitudes endemic to those societies. On the one hand utilitarianism, which sees pleasure as the goal of human action, but as external to those actions which are a mere means to it, just as alienated labour is a means to pleasures external to it that the wages earned can buy. As against this, Marx is insisting that, in truly human conditions, it is activity itself which is fulfilling – pleasure is not an external end but, as for Aristotle, 'unimpeded activity'. And this activity is often of an intrinsically social nature, not an egoistic one.

On the other hand, Kant, unlike almost all pre-capitalist moral philosophers, sees happiness as in no sense the goal of morality: rather, the impulse to happiness must be sacrificed to dutiful activity for its own sake, a morality which resembles that of Marx's ascetic but productive slave.

As to the 'truly human conditions' which I referred to, they are of course communism. But communism 'at first appears' (presumably in the ideology of early communist sects) 'as universal private property' (*Early Writings*, p. 346). By this Marx seems to mean that while communal ownership replaces private, the relation of the (collective) proprietor to the property is the same as that of a private owner to private property: it is a possessive relationship. This, says Marx, 'threatens to destroy *everything* which is not capable of being possessed by everyone as private property; it wants to abstract from talent, etc., by *force*' (*Early Writings*, p. 346). This 'crude and unthinking' communism desires 'to level everything down' and negates 'the entire world of culture and civilisation'. It replaces marriage by making women 'common property', 'the prey and handmaid of communal lust' (*Early Writings*, p. 347). Marx goes on to say that the nature of the relationship between man and woman is the clue to any society's level of humanity.

> It therefore demonstrates the extent to which man's *natural* behaviour has become *human* or the extent to which his *human* essence has become a *natural* essence for him, the extent to which his *human nature* has become *nature* for him. This relationship also demonstrates the extent to which man's *needs* have become *human* needs, hence the extent to which the *other*, as a human being, has become a need for him, the extent to which in his most individual existence he is at the same time a communal being. (*Early Writings*, p. 347)

Against the crude type of communism (which one feels Marx must have encountered in some of the sects around at the time, since he writes of it with such animus), Marx presents an ideal of communism which is no longer defined negatively, in terms of the type of society it is superseding, but is a positive affirmation of humanity. This is, he says, 'the positive supersession of all estrangement, and the return of man from religion, the family, the state, etc., to his *human*, i.e. his *social* existence' (*Early Writings*, p. 349).

Although Marx writes several pages on this humanistic communism, he cannot be said to give a very clear picture of it: only that all activities will be fulfilments of the human essence and all will be in some sense social, even those, like scientific work (that is, theoretical work) which are carried out alone. Also, that our relation to things will not be proprietary. Under present conditions as we have seen, 'Private property has made us so stupid and one-sided that an object is only *ours* when we have it, when it exists for us as capital or when we directly possess, eat, drink, wear, inhabit it, etc., in short, when we *use* it' (p. 351). Under communism, 'Need or enjoyment have therefore lost their *egoistic* nature, and nature has lost its mere *utility* in the sense that its use has become *human* use' (p. 352).

But despite Marx's intention of presenting communism as positive humanism, and not in contrast with present conditions, it is in fact only that contrast which gives his picture what concreteness it has. In later writings, he will treat this as a virtue: we can say what needs to be abolished, but the details of what is to replace it must be left to the people of that time.

Nevertheless, Marx has clearly arrived in these manuscripts at several of the conclusions that he was to hold throughout his life: that capitalism exploits the workers; that it inverts the relation of producer to product, making the product dominate the producer; that the only solution to these problems is the common ownership of the means of labour. However, he did not work these manuscripts up into publishable form nor did he use several of their central concepts in his published works. Concepts like 'alienation', 'the human essence' and 'species-being' disappear, while concepts like 'the capitalist mode of production', 'surplus value' and 'class struggle' appear. He is even at times explicitly critical of his earlier concepts. For instance in *The Communist Manifesto* he writes of the inferiority of German socialist philosophizing to hard-headed French political writing:

> They wrote their philosophical nonsense beneath the French original. For instance, beneath the French criticism of the economic functions of money, they wrote 'alienation of humanity', and beneath the French criticism of the bourgeois state they wrote, 'dethronement of the category of the general' and so forth ... The French socialist and communist literature was thus completely emasculated. And since it ceased in the hands of the German to express the struggle of one class with the other, he felt conscious of having overcome 'French one-sidedness' and of representing, not true requirements, but the requirements of truth; not the interests of the proletariat, but the interests of human nature, of man in general, who belongs to no class, has no reality, who exists only in the misty realm of philosophical fantasy. (*The Revolutions of 1848*, p. 91)

Has there then been a sharp break between the young and the mature Marx, as for instance Louis Althusser argues (see his *For Marx*)? I think there is a break, but many things are not jettisoned. Marx's comment on money, for example, as 'the universal pimp of men and peoples' (*Early Writings*, p. 377) is echoed by the statement in *The Communist Manifesto* that the bourgeoisie 'has resolved personal worth into exchange value' (*The Revolutions of 1848*, p. 70), and by numerous statements in his economic writings. Likewise, his critique of the proprietary attitude to nature is echoed in *Capital*, vol. 3 where he says that even the whole of humankind does not 'own' the Earth, but each generation must leave it in as good condition as they found it (1981, p. 911). And as I have said, the exposure of what capitalism does to the workers, and the theme of producer–product inversion, persist throughout his work.

But there are real problems with Marx's early work, and they are not just literary (for which he cannot be blamed, since he did not intend to publish them).

In the first place, there is the question of method: what is the essential focus of social science? A quote from an earlier text gives the clue to the young Marx's view: 'To be radical is to grasp things by the root; but for man the root is man himself' (quoted by Louis Althusser, *For Marx*, p. 226). Humankind is the essential focus of the EPM. While the difference between humankind under conditions of alienation and humankind freed from those conditions is a central theme, the variety of modes of production – for instance the relation of capitalism to feudalism – is not studied; nor is the origin of capitalism. The nearest Marx gets to a discussion of the relation between feudalism and capitalism is his account (*Early Writings*, pp. 338–9) of the mutual opinions of landlords and capitalists: capitalists see landlords as lazy, unenlightened halfwits while landlords see capitalists as heartless money-grubbers who destroy all communal ties – and Marx thinks neither is lying.

It is as if humankind is the agent in history, and it alienates itself, that is, the alienating is its action. Yet it is very much the action of some people against others, and of the structures which allow some people to oppress others. In a very late text of Marx, he offers an alternative account of method: 'My analytical method does not start from man but from the economically given social period' (quoted by Louis Althusser, *For Marx*, p. 219). And this is true of Marx's mature works. He no longer wrote about how men and women in general behave, but how they must behave so long as they are workers or capitalists. This brings about a great gain in specificity and exactness.

There is an ethical dimension to this as well, in terms of human ideals. Marx's early humanism contrasts our humanity with our specific descriptions (for example, as a Frenchman, a carpenter, a husband, and so on), and sees the humanity itself as the important thing – indeed suggests that we are alienated in these roles ('return from religion, family, the state etc., to his *human* i.e. *social* existence'). But someone might say (as Hegel would have said): but my religion, family, state etc. *is* my social existence, that is where I am fulfilled. Actually, Marx himself made fun of this rather reductive humanist cult of unspecificity later in *The German Ideology*:

> All quibbles about names are resolved in humanism; wherefore communists, wherefore socialists? We are human beings – *tous frères, tous amis* ... Wherefore human beings, wherefore beasts, wherefore plants, wherefore stones? We are bodies! (*The German Ideology*, ed. Pascal, p. 94)

There is another issue about this humanist ideal as well. Marx may be right that what distinguishes the human species is productive labour. But why should what distinguishes the human from the animal be more important for the human ideal than what we share with the animals? Granted that productive work can be fulfilling, and in a good society would be much more so than it is now, is there not a place too for more passive pleasures? Paul Lafargue once wrote a book called *The Right to be Lazy* (*Droit de la Paresse*). Should not socialism also make room for this right?

Finally, although there are environmentalist themes in the young Marx, they remain anthropocentric: we ought to care for nature because it is our inorganic body; we ought to be aware of non-utilitarian values in nature because our senses are impoverished without them. It has been objected that one of the differences between nature and our bodies is that we have lots of rights over our own bodies that we do not have over anything else. I can shave my hair off if I like, but I ought not to be able to cut down the rainforest if I like.

Certainly Marx means the idea of nature as our inorganic body to entail care for nature rather than wilful or irresponsible use of it, but certainly also, insofar as Marx is an environmentalist, it is of the 'shallow ecology' sort, not 'deep ecology', that is, he thinks we should look after the environment because it is *our* environment rather than because it has intrinsic worth.

For the last forty years, the EPM has had much more appeal than other texts by Marx. It obviously strikes a cord in the imagination of very modern humankind. The question arises whether it is particularly relevant to the modern world. Yet, as much as *Capital*, its empirical descriptions of workers' conditions do not match with the experience of workers in industrialized countries today: who – in those countries – now 'has only one need left – the need to *eat*, to eat *potatoes*, and, more precisely, to eat *rotten potatoes*, the worst kind of potatoes' (*Early Writings*, p. 360)?

Yet the experience of alienation as defined by Marx – of one's time being stolen from one, of one's product turning against one, of work being only an undesirable means to an external end – seems widespread. Perhaps, while material conditions have improved, alienation has taken over even areas of life that escaped it in Marx's day. The defining cases of unalienated work (artistic production, cooking a meal for one's family or friends) – work in which one has no boss, possesses the means of labour, and works for the sake of the finished product and the pleasure it will give others, not the money it will bring in – have increasingly been edged out of that position. Art becomes the design market, cooking is replaced by working extra alienated time to pay for ready meals. Education is increasingly dominated by assessment, and reduced to uncreative cramming. Even in a university, to suggest that learning may have a value in itself is to invite derision. To use a distinction made recently by the French Socialist Party, we have not just a market economy, but a market society. Even marriage has come to be seen as a contract. In this ideological climate where the spirit of commerce pervades every sphere of life, the indignation of the young Marx against the prostitution of humanity is as appropriate as ever.

Chapter Three

Towards a Science of History

> The philosophers have only *interpreted* the world, in various ways; the point is to *change* it. (*Early Writings*, p. 423)

These words, the 'eleventh thesis on Feuerbach', that Marx jotted down for self-clarification in 1845, are perhaps the most quoted and the most misunderstood words of Marx. It is possible that Marx had in mind the words of Hegel that 'the owl of Minerva spreads its wings only with the falling of the dusk', that is, that philosophy comes at the end of an epoch, and understands that epoch, but does not help prepare a new one. In which case, Marx's remark bears comparison with that of his fellow critic of Hegel (with whom he shared a birthday), Sören Kierkegaard: 'It is true that life can only be understood backwards; but it can only be lived forwards.' But Marx wants an understanding that can help us live forwards.

However, Marx is not asking for a philosophy that will provide us with this understanding. Since the saying is a thesis on Feuerbach, it is presumably rejecting Feuerbach's philosophy as well as Hegel's – and hence also Marx's own, very Feuerbachian, philosophy of the EPM. He is in fact not proclaiming a new philosophy that will change the world, but in some measure turning his back on philosophy altogether, as not being the kind of knowledge that can help us change the world. Later, as we shall see, Marx returns to philosophy in some of his methodological forewords to his economic writings; but it is a humbler sort of philosophy – a philosophy that acts as an underlabourer for social science, rather than legislating for it.

For if Marx is turning away from philosophy with this saying, it is to social science that he is turning. Thesis eleven certainly does not mark a turning away from theory in general, to a life of action. All Marx's greatest theoretical work was yet to come when he wrote this. His other main work of 1845, *The German Ideology*, sketches out a programme for a social science, or, as Marx would prefer to call it, a science of history. Not history in the sense of the past, but in the sense of the development of human societies, past, present and future.

Perhaps it is necessary to say first what Marx's theory of history is not. It is not a theory of inevitable stages through which history must pass. It is often thought that Marx believed that there were five inevitable successive stages in history: primitive communal, slavery, feudalism, capitalism, socialism. Marx did think that, in Europe at least, we had passed through the first four of these 'modes of production' as he calls them, and that the fifth was now on the agenda. But the non-inevitability of this succession is shown by Marx's idea that in some Asian countries a different mode of production had occurred, roughly parallel with feudalism in Europe, which he called the Asiatic mode of production. This did not have the seeds of capitalist development in it, as European feudalism did, and consequently was not replaced by capitalism as a result of internal development, but only because of its encounter with the imperialism of the capitalist West. Likewise, towards the end of his life, he envisaged the possibility that Russia might skip the capitalist stage and pass straight from the village commune or *mir*, to socialism.

In fact Marx's theory of history is not any kind of overview, but an idea about what, within any mode of production, makes history develop in the way that it does. The key issue is the relation of humankind to the means of labour. There are two aspects of this, which it is convenient to call the horizontal and vertical aspects. Horizontally, our relations with the means of labour alter in the course of history as the means of labour themselves alter. The relation of a flint knife, a blast furnace and a computer to their users is necessarily very different. Herein lies the secret of the fact that history is a development, in which each stage presupposes the last and makes possible the next, not just 'one damned thing after another'. Vertically, history is the history of class struggle, where the classes are constituted precisely by their relations to the means of labour. In slavery, the workers, like their means of labour, are the property of the master. In feudalism, the serf is guaranteed a plot of land (his main means of labour) on condition that he works unpaid for the lord of the manor on that lord's land. In capitalism, the proletarian is legally free, that is, owns his own labour power, but does not own the means of labour, and therefore must sell his labour power to the capitalist, who does own them. In a socialist mode of production, the workers own their own means of labour collectively. Slavery, feudalism and capitalism have in common that there is a class exploiting the workers, that is, taking a portion of their product by virtue of their control over the means of labour, and consequently that there is a conflict of interests, and class struggle, between the workers and the exploiters.

The programme for research into history as a science is set out in Part I of *The German Ideology*, written in 1845 by Marx and Engels. The distinctive features of their approach in this text are: (1) the idea that, 'Life is not determined by consciousness, but consciousness by life' (*The German Ideology*, ed. C.J. Arthur, p. 47), so that the starting point of social science should not be people's ideas but the way they live their lives; (2) that the crucial facts about how they live their lives are how they produce their means of life from nature, and what relations with other people this involves; (3) there is a strong strain of what might be called individualism in this text. This involves both scepticism about talk of 'society as the subject' or history as a 'person ranking with other persons' (*The German Ideology*, pp. 55, 57), both of which ideas Marx and Engels make fun of, and also the anarchist-sounding claim that the proletarians 'to assert themselves as individuals ... must overthrow the state' (p. 85); (4) there first appears here the notion of history as periodized by several great 'modes of production', ancient, feudal, capitalist and so on; (5) there is a stress on the liberating potential of technology, and the need for certain levels of technology as a condition without which liberation is impossible: 'slavery cannot be abolished without the steam-engine and the mule and spinning-jenny' and so on (p. 61); (6) there is a much greater stress than in later texts on the division of labour, which almost takes the place that alienation had in the works of the previous year, and is seen both as the original source of class divisions, and as due to be abolished under communism, though one cannot be sure how seriously they meant the following passage:

> In communist society ... society regulates the general production and thus makes it possible for me to do one thing today and another tomorrow, to hunt in the morning, fish in the afternoon, rear cattle in the evening, criticise after dinner, just as I have a mind, without ever becoming hunter, fisherman, shepherd or critic. (p. 53)

This is not a theme that recurs in Marx's later writings, though he remained critical of the tendency of capitalism to make people one-sided by development of a too narrow range of talents. (The recent publication of the text of *The German Ideology* showing what is in Marx's and what in Engels's handwriting has been read by Terrell Carver as showing that Marx was expressing scepticism at Engels's use of this rather Fourierist image of communism. But I suspect that, while neither expected to be taken literally, both genuinely thought at this time that the division of labour harmed people by narrowing their potential. See Carver's *Postmodern Marx*, pp. 99–107.)

It is important to get clear at the outset what Marx means by the various classes, particularly under capitalism. They are all defined by their relation to the means of labour, and to each other with respect to their means of labour. A capitalist, or 'bourgeois' (in the strictest sense of the word), owns the means of labour, buys the power of the proletarians to operate those means, and sells the product; a prole-tarian does not own the means of labour, and so has to sell his or her labour power to the capitalist to gain access to those means. The means of labour include land, tools and raw materials. Those work-ers who own means of labour individually and work them on their own account, Marx calls 'petty bourgeois'. He believed this class to be on the decline.

Marx does not use cultural criteria for class membership – educa-tion, lifestyle, accent or that sort of thing. Hence on the face of it any-one dependent on wages or salaries for their living is a proletarian, and will not be employed unless the capitalist can profit from their employment. However, income that is legally salary may in essence be profit, in the case of the director of a firm for instance. Even managers may be paid extra salary for their service of the employer's interest against the workers, over above what they earn by the sort of management skills that would be necessary even in a non-exploitive society. Managers may therefore not be proletarians, and are best regarded as belonging to an intermediate stratum, akin to the petty bourgeoisie. Many modern Marxists call such intermediate strata 'the new petty bourgeoisie' to distinguish them from the traditional self-employed petty bourgeoisie. It is worth noting that Marx regarded the increasing division between ownership and management, as shareholders replaced individual mill owners and salaried managers took over their managerial functions, as showing the social redundancy of the capitalist class, preparing the way for socialism. Anti-Marxists often allege that this development of separate ownership and management has somehow made Marxism obsolete, but in fact Marx was one of the first to notice it and predict its future prevalence.

Now we come to the relation between the horizontal and the vertical dimensions of history. Even the type of grain used in a particular region of the world can affect the social structure: rice needs a more collective effort to grow than wheat, and hence rice-growing societies have more collective forms of organization than wheat-growing ones. The relations between the worker, the exploiter and the means of labour are different in each mode of production, and the difference can partly be explained by the different means of labour in each mode of production. For the modes of production typically correspond to stages in the development of the means of labour, technological levels. Feudalism works when the main means of labour is land, tools being relatively simple. It could not work in a factory, because a factory could not be divided up into workers' and boss's plots, like the land of a feudal village can. So change in the vertical dimension of history – the relations between classes – is caused by horizontal development in the means of labour.

But while the means of labour progress slowly and steadily, change in class relations is structural change, and tends to take the form of a sharper break, often a revolution. In the past, such revolutions have resulted in a new exploiting class, more suited to more advanced means of labour, replacing the old ones. Foremost in Marx's mind is the transition from feudalism to capitalism, which was recent history, culminating in the French revolution – indeed it was not yet complete in parts of Europe.

While the means of labour not only change but progress, in that with new techniques one can do more, or do the same in less time, it might look from what I have said so far that in the vertical dimension – relations of class exploitation – there is change but no progress, in that one set of exploiters replaces another. A striking passage near the beginning of *The Communist Manifesto* seems to support this:

> The history of all hitherto existing society is the history of class struggles.
>
> Freeman and slave, patrician and plebeian, lord and serf, guild-master and journeyman, in a word, oppressor and oppressed, stood in constant opposition to one another, carried on an uninterrupted, now hidden, now open fight, a fight that each time ended, either in a revolutionary reconstitution of society at large, or in the common ruin of the contending classes. (*The Revolutions of 1848*, pp. 67–8)

But it is not Marx's view that this succession involves no progress in freedom for the worker. Certainly the capitalists, like the feudal lords, are exploiters. But they are not only better suited to managing factories and more capable of fostering technical progress; their system also amounts to a genuine gain in workers' freedom. The superior technology itself means that there is potentially more free time left over after society has produced its necessities. The legal freedom of the worker means that he or she can, subject to work being available, change employers. Certainly workers at the time of the transition from feudalism to capitalism preferred the status of wage labourers to that of serfs; they risked the penalties of the law to run away from their village and sell their services as a wage labourer to another lord in another village. Marx definitely saw the bourgeois revolutions that replaced feudalism by capitalism as stages in the history of human liberation, even though, of course, not the final stage. In *The Communist Manifesto* he shows a certain ambivalence towards the ruling class of capitalist society, the bourgeoisie. On the one hand, it has 'accomplished wonders far surpassing Egyptian pyramids, Roman aqueducts, and Gothic cathedrals'; on the other hand it has 'left remaining no other nexus between man and man than naked self-interest, than callous "cash payment"' (*The Revolutions of 1848*, p. 70). There is a certain 'heartlessness' about capitalism in comparison with feudalism, in that it is an impersonal system in which no one is his brother's keeper, while the feudal lord was supposed to be a protector of his serfs; but that personal responsibility was bought at the price of personal dependence. The bourgeoisie has not just achieved wonders of technology, it has, up to a point, liberated people. Hence Marx always sides with the bourgeoisie against the remnants of European feudalism. Not all Marxists have agreed. William Morris tended to regard the period in the fifteenth century between the end of serfdom and the Tudor enclosures as the golden age of the English working class, though of course he was quite aware that it was still exploited in this period. But in one sense this was already capitalism, since the workers were either tenants or wage labourers, not serfs. But it was a capitalism with a feudal feel to it.

Here a few words about Marx's terminology are required. The term 'the working class' is the most natural in English to refer to those exploited under capitalism. But of course all societies have a working class, whether they are slaves, serfs or wage labourers; and indeed the petty bourgeoisie under capitalism also live by their work. Hence Marx uses the technical term 'proletarian' for those whose only means of livelihood is to sell their labour power. The word has an interesting origin. In a war in ancient Rome, the propertied classes could send their horses to the war, but the propertiless had no horses and could only send their sons. Hence they were called 'proletarians' from *proles*, an offspring. In capitalism, proletarians are those who contribute their own flesh and blood to the production process, rather than their possessions.

Here we need to introduce another pair of phrases which are technical terms in Marx: the 'forces of production' and the 'relations of production'. The forces of production comprise the means of labour (land, tools and raw materials) and the workers themselves with their various skills appropriate to specific means of labour. Thus the forces of production are the economic resources of society, including what today are cynically called 'human resources'. The relations of production are relations between these various forces of production, and between them and their exploiters; relations for instance between workers and means of labour (a relation of non-ownership under capitalism), between capitalist and means of labour (a relation of ownership), and between worker and capitalist (a relation of sale of labour power). Forces of production and relations of production can only be separated in thought, because forces are always related by relations, and relations are always relations between forces. But they can be distinguished in thought, and it can be said that in some ways the nature of the forces of production in a given society explains the relations of production in that society. As we have seen, factories make feudal relations impossible, and so give you capitalism.

However, this explanation of relations of production by forces of production is of a special kind. For of course, factories did not first appear and then give rise to capitalists: capitalists had the factories built. The point is rather that when technology in the means of labour reached a certain point, it became necessary to have capitalist relations of production if the technology was to be used. In a certain sense, society became capitalist in order that it could build factories, in much the way that one might say that birds have hollow bones in order to aid flight. This does not of course mean that the ancestors of birds thought 'we'd better acquire hollow bones, or our descendants won't be able to fly'. Likewise, no one said 'we'd better establish capitalism, or our descendants won't have factories'. But proto-birds that had hollow bones caught their prey or escaped their predators and therefore passed on their genes, which those without hollow bones did not. Likewise, wherever pockets of capitalism occurred within feudal society, technological progress speeded up, and so these pockets grew until they were strong enough to supplant feudalism. So the 'in order to' clauses above should not be read as implying purpose. They mark what G.A. Cohen has called 'consequence explanations' (in his *Marx's Theory of History: a Defence*). That is, it is because their hollow bones have the consequence that birds can fly, that birds have hollow bones; it is because capitalism has the consequence that technology progresses fast, that capitalism prevails.

(The notion of consequence explanations is of course contentious, like everything else in philosophy. For a criticism of Cohen, see Ted Honderich 'Against Teleological Historical Materialism', *Inquiry*, 25, 1982; see also my reply in my *Socialist Reasoning*, pp. 24–8.)

Hence, in saying that the forces of production explain the relations of production, Marx is not saying that relations of production have no effects on forces of production. On the contrary, it is only because relations of production do have effects of forces of production (for instance, capitalism promotes technical growth), that forces of production in the long run explain relations of production (capitalism prevails because it promotes technical growth).

Something similar is true in the other contexts in which Marx talks about the 'base' and 'superstructure' of society. He likens the economic structure to the foundation upon which other aspects of society, for instance politics and ideology, are built. It is not always clear from Marx's own writing how many 'storeys' he thinks there are, but I think there is much to be said for the account given by Plekhanov, the founder of Russian Marxism and the teacher of Lenin (though he opposed the Russian Revolution as premature). Plekhanov lists five levels, starting from the most basic and finishing with the most superstructural:

1. the state of the productive forces;
2. the economic relations these forces condition;
3. the socio-political system that has developed on the given economic 'basis';
4. the mentality of social man, which is determined in part directly by the economic conditions obtaining, and in part by the entire socio-political system that has arisen on that foundation;
5. the various ideologies that reflect the properties of that mentality. (*Selected Philosophical Works*, vol. III, pp. 167–8)

Each of these levels in some way explains those that are higher; however, this does not mean that the higher levels have no effects on the lower. For instance, Marx's whole conception of socialist revolution is of a political revolution transforming the relations of production.

The point is rather that the more basic levels explain how the higher levels can have effects. There is an interesting comment on this in a footnote to *Capital*:

> My view is that each particular mode of production, and the relations of production corresponding to it at each given moment, in short 'the economic structure of society', is 'the real foundation, on which arises a legal and political superstructure and to which correspond definite forms of social consciousness', and that 'the mode of production of material life conditions the general process of social, political and intellectual life'.
>
> In the opinion of the German-American publication this is all very true for our own times, in which material interests are predominant, but not for the Middle Ages, dominated by Catholicism, nor for Athens and Rome, dominated by politics ... One thing is clear: the Middle Ages could not live on Catholicism, nor could the ancient world on politics. On the contrary, it is the manner in which they gained their livelihood which explains why in one case politics, in the other case Catholicism, played the chief part. (*Capital*, vol. 1, 1976, pp. 174–6, n. 35)

Here Marx is accepting that something other than the economic base 'played the chief part' in certain societies, that is, presumably, had more pronounced effects on the society than anything else. But this fact itself needs explanation, and the explanation for it is to be found in the way people 'gained their livelihood'. Perhaps the fact that exploitation under feudalism is transparent, in that the serf knows exactly how many days he or she works for the lord of the manor and how many days on their own plot of land, means that the relations of production under feudalism do not seem self-justifying, as those under capitalism do to those who believe their wages are payment for their labour; so an ideology separate from the production process itself is required to reconcile the peasants with their lot. Or, more simply, there is the fact that, by the end of the Middle Ages, the Church owned about a third of the land.

There seem to be two degrees of explanation here: on the one hand, the different levels have effects on the process of history that are in no fixed proportion, but differ from society to society; on the other, each of these levels is itself explained by the more basic levels.

The view that economics in the last analysis explains ideology rather than vice versa is a contentious opinion of Marx. Recent disputes between historians of the French revolution are largely between Marxist historians, who see it as essentially a class struggle, and non-Marxists, who see the determinants of the political struggles as being in the ideology of various groups rather than their economic class positions. Another classic confrontation between Marx and an alternative explanation concerns the relation between Protestantism and capitalism. Both sides in this dispute say that there is some such relation. Protestantism appealed to the early bourgeoisie of the German free cities and the maritime nations, and, in its Calvinist or Puritan form, became the ideology that steeled bourgeois revolutions in Scotland, Holland and England.

But which is cause and which effect? The German sociologist Max Weber argued (in his book *The Protestant Ethic and the Spirit of Capitalism*) that Protestantism caused capitalism. Crudely, the mechanism is like this: the Protestants valued hard work and abstinence from superfluities, as 'good for the soul'; they therefore accumulated capital and became, willy-nilly, successful capitalists. Catholicism by contrast had, on the one hand, with its numerous holidays on saints' days, permitted greater idleness, and on the other, poured the fruits of its abstinence into ecclesiastical foundations rather than ploughing them back into industry. So wherever Protestantism flourished, capitalism followed. Marx would not deny that Protestantism aided the development of capitalism, but would say that it was because capitalism was already emerging that Protestantism was selected for – whereas earlier heresies that prefigured Protestantism, such as the Lollards in England and the Hussites in the Czech lands, had no emerging capitalist class to take them up, and so were defeated. One might also claim that Protestantism was itself transformed (as Catholicism was at a later date) by being hijacked by capitalism. Early Protestants, as Tawney shows in his *Religion and the Rise of Capitalism*, were not advocates of unbridled capitalism. While Calvin permitted usury (interest on the loan of money) which medieval Catholicism, like orthodox Islam today, denounced, he did try to limit it. In Geneva, under his rule, you could not take interest from a poor person. He also established minimum wages and maximum prices. Martin Luther was even less favourable to the essential capitalist institution of usury. Marx quotes him on this:

> The heathen were able, by the light of reason, to conclude that a usurer is a double-dyed thief and murderer. We Christians, however, hold them in such honour, that we fairly worship them for the sake of their money ... Whoever eats up, robs, and steals the nourishment of another, that man commits as great a murder (so far as in him lies) as he who starves a man or utterly undoes him. Such does a usurer, and sits the while safe on his stool, when he ought rather to be hanging on the gallows, and be eaten by as many ravens as he has stolen guilders, if only there were so much flesh on him, that so many ravens could stick their beaks in and share it ... And since we break on the wheel, and behead, highwaymen, murderers, and housebreakers, how much more ought we to break on the wheel and kill ... hunt down, curse and behead all usurers. (*Capital*, vol. 1, 1976, p. 740, n. 22)

It should be said that this quote from the founder of the Protestant religion is the only place in *Capital* where such violent sentiments are expressed.

But this anti-capitalist strain in early Protestantism was soon abandoned by all but a few radical sects. I suggest that the fact that Protestantism was taken over by capitalism in this way suggests that Marx's hypothesis is stronger than Weber's.

In recent times, many within Marxism have wanted to drop this base-superstructure model. It is criticized as merely metaphorical, as if this made it unscientific. Of course, 'base' and 'superstructure' started life as metaphors. But so did all scientific terms: 'wave' in physics, 'market' in economics, 'follows' in logic, 'square' in mathematics, and so on. The Marxist classical scholar George Thomson argues (in his book *The First Philosophers*) that all abstract terms must start as metaphors from concrete ones. But these erstwhile metaphors lose their metaphorical nature as soon as they are given a rigorous sense within a science – and likewise for 'base' and 'super-structure'. I think the discontent with these terms is partly due to the feeling that, once it is admitted that the superstructure has effects on the base, neither can really be causally prior, or it is just a matter of degree – of the base having *more* effects on the superstructure than vice versa. But this is not so: the way in which all levels affect all others in history is different from the way in which the lower levels explain the higher. It is rather like the relation between chemistry and biology. The chemical structure of DNA molecules explains biological inheritance, not the other way round; but biological events leave their traces in the non-biological world, through the action of plants and animals, just as the chemical world leaves its traces on the biological. If Lovelock is to be believed, it is an effect as well as a condition of life on Earth that the planet still contains hydrogen. The base-superstructure model does not say that history is affected more by economics than by politics or ideology, but that the way that politics and ideology have their effects is explained by economic considerations (for instance, politics and ideology are always class politics and ideology, and class is defined economically).

What recent Marxists (for instance, Louis Althusser) have liked least is the idea that the forces of production explain the relations of production. They will accept that politics and ideology are founded on economics, but they will insist on the primacy of the social (relations of production) over the technical (forces of production). A case can be made on both sides of this dispute, but I think there is no doubt which Marx is on. The fact that he believed that the electric motor would destroy capitalism illustrates that. Of course, he was wrong about the electric motor, but not that technical progress could destroy the system. The current environmental crisis suggests that either people will destroy capitalism as a condition of using technology responsibly, or the effects of technology will destroy capitalism by destroying life on Earth.

Since Marx claims to have inaugurated a science of history, certain expectations may be aroused about his theory that are misleading. In the positivist culture of the English-speaking world, it is commonly held that science has to have something to do with prediction. In passing, it can be said that this is less so for German speakers, for whom Marx initially wrote. In German, the title 'science' (or *Wissenschaft*) can quite naturally be applied to any rigorous discipline that takes us beyond everyday knowledge, be it literary criticism or theology. But, in the English-speaking world, 'science' evokes images of experimental sciences, and predictions are expected to be made for two reasons: firstly, it is thought that a science can only be proved by the accuracy of its predictions; and secondly, it is asked what practical use a science can have if it is not predictive. I shall discuss the question of predictions in the science of history later, in connection with a paradox that is supposed to arise about them. Here I only want to point out that Marx's conception of history could be a science, and a useful one, without any predictions.

First of all, experimental sciences are judged by their predictions in one context only: the predicted results of their experiments. But the science of history is not an experimental science. Neither, for example, is Darwin's evolutionary theory. Yet that theory has great explanatory power, without making any predictions at all. And that is the theory to which Engels, in his speech at Marx's funeral, compares Marx's theory.

Secondly, as to the practical use of a non-predictive science. Marx's theory certainly gives grounds for holding that there are various constraints on what can happen in history. One cannot establish a classless income distribution while property in the means of production is still a class monopoly, for instance. Some 'analytical philosophy' critics of Marx have suggested that one could pass straight from capitalism to 'communism', without a 'socialist' stage, by taxing a still capitalist economy to provide an adequate 'citizen's income' for everyone. Perhaps one hardly needs Marx's theory to show this to be a non-starter: it is enough to quote the saying that I think comes from R.H. Tawney, 'You can peel an onion leaf by leaf, but you can't skin a live tiger claw by claw.' But Marx's theory certainly does rule out this possibility. Thus the theory provides a set of constraints on the transformation of society, which tell you 'how not to do it'. It may also reveal some constraints on the reproduction of society: capitalism cannot go on reproducing itself indefinitely without generating self-destructive tendencies. Of this, too, more later.

Finally I would like to end this chapter by looking at Marx's theory of history at work via concrete analysis of a historical situation, in Marx's account of the revolution in France in 1848, and its aftermath, Napoleon III's seizure of power. The texts in which Marx discusses this are *Class Struggles in France 1848–1850* and *The Eighteenth Brumaire of Louis Bonaparte.*

In these texts, Marx is tracing the conflicts between classes, which led to the rise and fall of the Second Republic. The classes are defined in economic terms: landowners, finance capitalists, industrial capitalists, petty bourgeoisie, peasantry, proletariat. Each has definite political movements corresponding to it. Roughly, the 'legitimists', supporters of the Bourbon monarchy, represent the landowners; the supporters of the Orleanist monarchy, which was overthrown in 1848, represent finance capital; the opposition within the Orleanist regime and later the moderate republicans represent the industrial bourgeoisie; the 'Mountain' – the party that looked back to the First Republic and the Jacobins – represent the petty bourgeoisie; the various socialist and communist clubs represent the proletariat. The peasantry had no party of their own, and shifted their support between various other classes, eventually becoming, for reasons discussed later, the backbone of Napoleon III's dictatorship. The degree of discontent felt at various times by the various classes is partly determined by economic events, for instance the recession of 1847, which makes the revolution possible, and later economic recovery. The crucial events are not just the street fights, elections and coups whereby power changes hands, but above all the shifting pattern of class alliances, and the good and bad reasons why a particular class at a particular time is friendly or hostile to another class.

The Orleanist monarchy of 1830–48, with its parliament elected by limited suffrage with a property qualification, is dominated by the bankers; the industrial bourgeoisie forms the basis of the opposition; other classes are excluded from political life. The revolution of February 1848 sets up a provisional government that is a coalition of all forces opposed to the bankers' dominance, and the proletarians, who bore the main brunt of the fighting, got two representatives in the government. However, the leading role of the workers, who force the provisional government to declare a republic based on manhood suffrage, leaves its initial mark on the new republic. They can do this because 'Paris, as a result of political centralization, rules France' and 'the workers, in moments of revolutionary earthquake, rule Paris'. However, the elections, which are nationwide, do not reflect this; the peasants do not see the proletarians as their natural allies, and the assembly elected in May 1848 is dominated by the bourgeois republicans, who can rely on the support of the Mountain to back republican institutions, and of the two royalist factions to impose order on the subject classes. The few concessions to the workers do not work to their favour in the long run. National Workshops are set up to provide a right to work, but Marx compares these to the hated English workhouses. Nevertheless, they were better than nothing for the workers who would otherwise be unemployed. But other classes, particularly the petty bourgeoisie, see them as scroungers at the taxpayers expense, much as the British petty bourgeoisie currently sees dole claimants. Moreover, a new tax imposed by the bourgeois republicans, which hits the peasants, is blamed by the latter on the proletarians, since they are the class most associated with the republic. Hence the proletariat becomes isolated from its potential allies, and when the government attacks the National Workshops and the workers revolt in June 1848, no one comes to their aid, and they are crushed with great bloodshed (over 3000 prisoners being massacred). Meanwhile, petty bourgeoisie and peasantry are being ruined by debt.

Peasant discontent, cut off from proletarian movements, expresses itself in support for Louis Napoleon ('the nephew of his uncle', as Marx calls him), who is elected president of the republic by a large majority in December 1848. When a new assembly is elected in May 1849, the royalist parties, united now as the 'Party of Order', are very strong in it, but since they cannot agree on a king, they accept the republic. The main opposition is now the combined forces of the petty bourgeois Mountain and the proletarian clubs, which together are known as Red Republicans or Social Democrats. However, after a victory for the left in the Paris by-elections in March 1850, the right-wing majority in the assembly votes to abolish manhood suffrage. The petty bourgeois leadership of the Social Democrats takes no decisive action against this. From then on, the remaining months of the republic are taken up by scheming of the president, Louis Napoleon, against the assembly and vice versa. In December 1851, the president overthrows his own assembly in a military coup, and makes himself emperor as Napoleon III.

Towards the end of *Class Struggles in France*, Marx explains one of the reasons for the failure of the revolution. The industrial bourgeoisie was underdeveloped relative to the finance capitalists. This not only meant that the proletariat was small, but that the financial fraction of the bourgeoisie was the most powerful, and generally got its way rather than the more progressive industrial capitalists. Hence the failure of the republican bourgeoisie to consolidate the support of the peasants by tax reform. Towards the end of *The Eighteenth Brumaire of Louis Bonaparte*, he discusses two other reasons: the overgrowth of the state apparatus in France through centralization, whether under monarchs or revolutionaries, which created the basis for Napoleon III's state, raised above society as a whole, even bourgeois society; and the nature of the peasantry as a class that could not organize itself:

> In so far as millions of families live under economic conditions of existence that divide their mode of life, their interests and their culture from other classes, and put them in hostile contrast to the latter, they form a class. In so far as there is merely a local interconnection among these small peasants, and the identity of their interests begets no unity, no national union and no political organisation, they do not form a class. They are consequently incapable of enforcing their class interest in their own name, whether through a parliament or through a convention. They cannot represent themselves, they must be represented. (*Selected Works in Two Volumes*, vol. 2, p. 415)

Hence, though the peasants had, in many areas, been revolutionary in the great French revolution under bourgeois leadership, they became the support of the bureaucratic regime of Napoleon III. This is because the bourgeoisie had alienated them, and they were not yet willing to throw in their lot with the proletariat. Their doing so would be a necessary condition of proletarian revolution succeeding, and that success would be a necessary condition of the peasants' emancipation from forms of exploitation to which they were still subject, mainly through indebtedness.

Scientific Socialism

Prior to Marx, most if not all socialist writers could be described as utopians. Their style of socialist advocacy was to write detailed constitutions for, or descriptions of, future or imaginary socialist societies. In some cases, for instance the eponymous *Utopia* of St Thomas More, it would be an exaggeration to call it socialist advocacy at all. It was a utopian fiction, an experiment in thought, which More had no intention of trying to realize. In other cases – Gerrard Winstanley, Etienne Cabet, Charles Fourier, Robert Owen – the idea was to set up utopian communities and convert people of goodwill by example.

It is quite natural that socialist advocacy should have taken this form. Non-socialist political philosophers generally gave advice about how existing kinds of state – monarchies or oligarchies – could best manage their affairs. Occasionally, as with Spinoza or Rousseau, they expressed a preference for democracy, but that preference remained utopian in the sense that neither had any idea how to get from where they were to these democratic states, and Spinoza even thought that it would be wrong to try to do so. Socialists could obviously not proceed in this way, and working out the best society for humans in general, and persuading people to support it, seemed the only alternative.

Marx had, I think, two objections to utopian socialism: a pragmatic one, that it gave no idea how to get from existing society to a socialist one; and a democratic one, that socialism must be the work of the mass of people, not the invention of some one intellectual, and that the present has no right to legislate for the future.

> The theoretical conclusions of the Communists are in no way based on ideas or principles that have been invented, or discovered, by this or that would-be universal reformer.
>
> They merely express, in general terms, actual relations springing from an existing class struggle, from a historical movement going on under our very eyes. ('Communist Manifesto', in *Selected Works in One Volume*, pp. 46–7)

The starting point then is a movement going on in existing society, which we can study with a view to discerning where it will lead if it succeeds. Likewise, Engels writes concerning the sexual morality of a future socialist society – a matter about which Fourier had very pronounced opinions – that all we can predict is what will be abolished, namely the economic power of men over women, after which people will work out their own morality appropriate to the new conditions, and 'will not care a rap about what we today think they should do' ('The Origin of the Family, Private Property and the State', in *Selected Works in One Volume*, p. 517).

Communism, then, for Marx, is not an ideal to be approximated to, but a movement of the working class which must have certain outcomes if it succeeds, whether or nor those outcomes are yet consciously intended. It is possible to predict certain broad features of those outcomes – the abolition of private property in the means of social production, for instance – but not to pre-empt the freedom of future generations to make history in their own way.

But if utopianism is renounced, what form does socialist advocacy take? The first thing it does is start from where we are, and ask what it is about where we are that makes it impossible to stay here. What makes it impossible, in Marx's terms, is contradictions. This is a technical term in Marx – it does not mean logical inconsistencies in what we say, as Marx makes very clear. A contradiction is a feature of some system which is dysfunctional for the system, yet which is an essential feature of the system. Class struggle is an essential part of capitalism, yet is dysfunctional to capitalism in that it leads to strikes and so on. Indeed it is so dysfunctional that a good deal of the function of the capitalist state is to try to eliminate this struggle, but this necessarily fails – class struggle can only cease when classes, and therefore capitalism itself, ceases. Likewise, the indifference of the driving forces of capitalism to environmental concerns is an essential feature of capitalism, yet it is so dysfunctional that it could destroy life on Earth, and presumably will if capitalism is not overthrown. So these contradictions are not just dysfunctional from a standpoint already opposed to the capitalist system, they are dysfunctional for the system itself, yet can only be abolished along with the system itself. Hence they can stand as objective reasons why the system should be superseded. And, given that they make life unpleasant or precarious for the victims of the system, they give masses of people a motive for abolishing the system – everyone, in fact, who has not got such a large pecuniary stake in the system that they cannot contemplate its demise. Only because contradictions can motivate large numbers of people against the system is it possible that the system can be abolished.

This notion of contradictions makes Marx unique in the history of political philosophy in that he both starts from where we are – from the existing system with its resources and people and contradictions – and yet derives from study of these existing beings and structures the need, not just for reform, but for revolutionary change. So,

> mankind always sets itself only such tasks as it can solve; since, looking at the matter more closely, it will always be found that the task itself arises only when the material conditions for its solution already exist or are at least in the process of formation. (1859 preface, *Selected Works in One Volume*, p. 183)

Attempting to realize a utopia for which existing conditions, and existing people, are not ready can only lead to disaster. As Engels comments of Thomas Münzer's role in the German peasant war at the time of the Reformation:

> The worst thing that can befall a leader of an extreme party is to be compelled to take over a government in an epoch when the

movement is not yet ripe for the domination of the class which he represents, and for the realization of the measures which that domination implies. What he *can* do depends not upon his will but upon the degree of contradiction between the various classes, and upon the level of development of the material means of existence, of the conditions of production and commerce upon which class contradictions always repose. (*The Peasant War in Germany*, pp. 138–9)

My own view is that to base politics on contradictions and subsequent avoidance of the alternatives of conservative pragmatics on the one hand, and on a utopian view from nowhere on the other, is one of Marx's greatest achievements, and by itself earns him the title of the greatest ever political thinker. It has been very little assimilated. Many people, including some who call themselves Marxists, still think that to radically criticize a society you have to take a standpoint outside that society. They do not recognize that a critique can be both internal to what it criticizes, and radical in its demands for transformation. Yet it is just such a critique that Marx invented.

Marx indicates his distance from utopian socialism by calling his own brand of socialism 'scientific'. This is an unpopular term today. People say that he called his theory scientific to claim infallibility for it, which is clearly wrong in that Marx and (more explicitly) Engels had a fallibilist conception of science. Marx would have agreed with Engels that,

science ... mounts from lower to ever higher levels of knowledge without ever reaching, by discovering so-called absolute truth, a point at which it can proceed no further ... Just as knowledge is unable to reach a complete conclusion in a perfect, ideal condition of humanity, so is history unable to do so; a perfect society, a perfect 'state', are things which can exist only in imagination. ('Ludwig Feuerbach and the End of Classical German Philosophy', in *Selected Works in One Volume*, p. 598)

Every scientific theory is fallible, and will probably one day be falsified, but we can learn more of the truth, without ever reaching 'the whole truth'. Scientific socialism, like every other scientific project, is fallible and subject to constant revision.

People dislike the term 'scientific socialism' because they think it is élitist. This goes back to Bakunin: reading Marx's conspectus of

Bakunin's *Statism and Anarchy*, we can see Bakunin's criticism and Marx's replies. Bakunin associates Marx's term 'scientific socialism' with the phrase 'educated socialism', which Marx points out he had never used. Marx goes on to say that the term 'scientific socialism' 'was used only in opposition to utopian socialism, which wants to attach the people to new delusions, instead of limiting its science to the knowledge of the social movement made by the people itself' (*The First International and After*, p. 337).

So utopian socialism fails to limit its science: it claims knowledge of how to organize a whole new society; scientific socialism makes more modest claims: to understand the movement of the people within existing society. Hence Marx writes three huge volumes on the economic laws of motion of capitalist society and scarcely as many pages on the economics of socialism.

Furthermore, Marx sees science as essentially communicable knowledge, which can be grasped by the people, as opposed to utopianism which expects the people to simply swallow the utopian ideal whole. This is shown by Marx's remarks to the German utopian socialist Weitling:

> To call to the workers without any strictly scientific ideas or constructive doctrine, especially in Germany, was equivalent to dishonest play at preaching which assumed on the one side an inspired prophet and on the other only gaping asses. (McLellan, *Karl Marx*, pp. 156–7)

In addition to this rejection of utopian politics in the strict sense – that is the depiction of concrete utopias to which we are urged to approximate – there is a style of political advocacy which is alien to Marx, though it is often seen as the essence of political philosophy. It shares with utopianism the attempt to judge societies from a standpoint outside history. This is the defence of policies as conducive to certain ideals, such as freedom, equality, justice or human rights. Marx's opposition to this kind of talk has often been misunderstood. It is not that there is an agreed content to these ideals, and that Marx rejects it. It is that none of these ideals generates a single set of policies. One cannot, for instance, be an advocate of freedom as such; freedom only exists as a multiplicity of freedoms, and some of these freedoms conflict with others. You can have freedom from slavery or freedom to own slaves, but not both; you can have freedom to use your car whenever you want or freedom to breathe clean air, but not both; you can have freedom of the press from censorship or freedom of the individual from persecution by the press, but not both; you can have freedom of residents to control the character of their neighbourhood or freedom of property developers to develop it, but not both. If you want freedoms at all, you must choose which freedoms you want, and which incompatible freedoms you reject.

Marx did not work out this idea with reference to freedom, but he did with reference to equality, in his *Critique of the Gotha Programme* (the Gotha Programme was the unification programme by which the German Social Democratic Party (SPD) was founded). He is criticizing the idea that 'the proceeds of labour belong, with equal right, to all members of society' (*Selected Works in One Volume*, p. 320). He comments:

> 'To all members of society'? To those who do not work as well? What remains then of the 'undiminished proceeds of labour'? Only to those members of society who work? What remains then of the 'equal right' of all members of society? (p. 322)

Marx goes on to generalize this argument:

> The right of the producers is *proportional* to the labour they supply; the equality consists in the fact that measurement is made with an *equal standard*, labour.
>
> But one man is superior to another physically or mentally and so supplies more labour in the same time, or can labour for a longer time; and labour, to serve as a measure, must be defined by its duration or intensity, otherwise it ceases to be a standard of measurement. This *equal* right is unequal for unequal labour. It recognises no class differences, because everyone is only a worker like everyone else; but it tacitly recognises unequal individual endowment and thus productive capacity as natural privileges. *It is, therefore, a right of inequality, in its content, like every right.* Right by its very nature can consist only in the application of an equal standard; but unequal individuals (and they would not be individuals if they were not unequal) are measurable only by an equal standard in so far as they are brought under an equal point of view, are taken from one *definite* side only, for instance, in the present case, are regarded *only as workers* and nothing more is seen in

them, everything else being ignored. Further, one worker is married, another not; one has more children than another, and so on and so forth. Thus, with equal performance of labour, and hence an equal share in the social consumption fund, one will in fact receive more than another, and so on. To avoid all these defects, right instead of being equal would have to be unequal. (p. 324)

The argument is essentially that equality is always equality in some respect: equal pay for equal work, or equal pay for equal needs, or indeed, from a capitalist point of view, equal right to a return from one's property. We have to choose which equality we want. We can no more favour equality in general than we can favour nationalism in general, since one's Welsh nationalism would conflict with one's British nationalism, and both with one's European nationalism, and so on.

Marx's own view on equality is that in the first stage of socialist society, the *main* criterion of pay will be work; but there will already be a 'social wage' of communal provision of education and health services, and this will grow as socialism develops (pp. 322–3). The tendency of this growth is towards a society where equal provision for equal needs replaces equal pay for equal work.

So socialism is not 'about equality' as is often said. It is about certain equalities: equal power over the means of production (common ownership), equal access to the means of production (right to work), equal availability of health care and education. It is against equal right to own or acquire property, equal opportunity to become an exploiter (which is what equal opportunity generally means today) – even against the strict application of equal pay for equal work, since this ignores differences of needs. Likewise, socialism is about certain freedoms: freedom to work, freedom from overwork, freedom of health care and education without financial barrier, freedom to share in control over one's working and living environment – as well as the general 'democratic liberties' such as freedom of speech, association, assembly, voting, and so on. But socialism would preclude freedom to invest, to employ the labour of others (on a large scale, at any rate), to buy and sell land or capital, to monopolize the media, to bribe politicians, and so on. I would also hope that socialism would give us very much more freedom to enjoy the environment and very much less freedom to pollute and destroy it than we have at present. Whether one would find a socialist society freer or less free than a capitalist society depends entirely on what one wants to do. I got much pleasure from my freedom to ramble across agricultural land in communist Hungary in 1970 – a freedom which I believe I would lack in many parts of the United States.

I think that some of Marx's replies to objections to communism in *The Communist Manifesto* are along the lines I have been indicating.

> We Communists have been reproached with the desire of abolishing the right of personally acquiring property as the fruit of a man's own labour, which property is alleged to be the groundwork of all personal freedom, activity and independence.
>
> Hard-won, self-acquired, self-earned property! Do you mean the property of the petty artisan and of the small peasant, a form of property that preceded the bourgeois form? There is no need to abolish that; the development of industry has to a great extent already destroyed it, and is still destroying it daily.
>
> Or do you mean modern bourgeois private property?
>
> But does wage labour create any property for the labourer? Not a bit. It creates capital, *i.e.*, that kind of property which exploits wage labour, and which cannot increase except on condition of begetting a new supply of wage-labour for fresh exploitation ...
>
> To be a capitalist, is to have not only a purely personal, but a social *status* in production. Capital is a collective product, and only by the united action of many members, nay, in the last resort, only by the united action of all members of society, can it be set in motion.
>
> Capital is, therefore, not a personal, it is a social power.
>
> When, therefore, capital is converted into common property, into the property of all members of society, personal property is not thereby transformed into social property. It is only the social character of the property that is changed. It loses its class character. (*Selected Works in One Volume*, p. 47)

In this passage, Marx is rebutting the charge that communism reduces 'the freedom of the individual'. It reduces the freedom that *some* individuals have by virtue of their power over others. It establishes for the first time the freedom of the individual worker. John Stuart Mill, who excluded the so-called 'economic liberties' from the list of liberties of the individual that he defended, could hardly have faulted Marx on this issue.

At this point it will be helpful to discuss the second sort of answer that Marx could give to the accusation that his proposals are 'against human nature'. We have seen that the young Marx had a conception of human nature that is both consistent with the facts of human motivation under capitalism, and compatible with the possibility of an advanced stage of communism. But, in order to defend the immediate socialist proposals that he advocates, it is not necessary to defend any contentious ideas about human nature at all. For these proposals could be implemented with people being exactly like they are now, under capitalism. The society that would exist after a socialist revolution would have a state, and would pay workers for work done. Hence one need not assume that people would have come to enjoy work, or to be completely altruistic, or that crime would have died out, to see that this society would be possible. For most people, the main difference would be that the threat of unemployment had been removed, that the working week was shorter, that they had more control over their working environment, and that health, housing and education services were better. It is difficult to see how anyone could imagine that these changes would shipwreck on human nature. To return to Marx's replies to objections:

> Communism deprives no man of the power to appropriate the products of society; all that it does is deprive him of the power to subjugate the labour of others by means of such appropriation.
>
> It has been objected that upon the abolition of private property all work will cease, and universal laziness will overtake us.
>
> According to this, bourgeois society ought long ago to have gone to the dogs through sheer idleness; for those of its members who work, acquire nothing, and those who acquire anything, do not work. (*Selected Works in One Volume*, p. 49)

Of course if people really are as Hobbes described them, and are so not just as a result of capitalism, but by nature, then the higher stage of communism that Marx sometimes talks about, where distribution is according to need and the state has withered away – the communism described in William Morris's *News from Nowhere* – could not come about. But a society that fell short of that, but was without unemployment, overwork, poverty, homelessness, fatally long hospital waiting times and ecological disasters, would be worth fighting for for its own sake.

Shortly I shall be looking at the concrete political programmes that Marx worked out at various times on the basis of this scientific socialism. But first a word about a fundamental feature of Marx's politics: the proletariat is always centre stage. Why should this be?

First of all, in relation to other classes. The proletariat, Marx argues, is the most exploited class, the class with 'radical chains', which therefore cannot emancipate itself without emancipating the whole of society. The petty bourgeoisie, on the other hand, naturally gravitates towards reforms that help it in its capacity as a class of small proprietors, and hence leave property (including bourgeois property) intact. The same is true of peasants when they own their own farms. Yet the emancipation of either of these classes from exploitation through rent and indebtedness is dependent on nationalizing the banks and rented land, which is typically part of the proletariat's political programme. Because of this, under favourable conditions, these classes can be won over to the side of the proletariat. But, when they act separately from the proletariat, they are easily deflected into support for bourgeois parties, which will keep them exploited. Furthermore, as we have seen, their atomized conditions of work make democratic organization by these classes very difficult, while proletarians naturally gravitate to democratic trade unions, and thence to class-conscious politics.

Furthermore, Marx assumed that all oppressed classes would more and more become part of the proletariat. By and large, that has happened. There are no peasants in the United Kingdom now, but there are rural proletarians. The supposed de-proletarianization that some claim to have occurred is largely illusory. It means little more than that most English proletarians would now look out of place in a Lowry painting. A proletarian with a degree, a mortgage and a car is still a proletarian. A secretary or a shopworker or a lorry driver is as much a proletarian as a miner or a steelworker. The shift from industrial to service employment in no way affects the class structure.

Secondly, there is now (quite rightly) much attention to forms of oppression along lines other than class, and (quite wrongly) the left today is so much more interested in the plight of women or racial minorities, that it has almost forgotten the proletarians, despite the fact that statistics on unequal opportunities in the United Kingdom show that the disadvantages suffered by a proletarian (even a white male one) are far greater than those suffered by a middle-class woman or member of a racial minority. It is symptomatic that in constitution-making in left organizations, one often encounters regulations providing special representation for women or racial minorities, never special representation for unemployed people or manual workers or homeless people, presumably because these last three categories are all within the proletariat, and the left is only interested in oppressed groups that have some middle-class members.

The modern left certainly neglects class, but did Marx neglect other forms of oppression? If by 'neglect' is meant 'think that they don't matter', the answer is clearly 'no'. He was certainly acutely aware of the oppression of Irish people, both by British rule in Ireland and by racism directed against Irish workers in English cities. (Engels of course was even more so, since his partner was a republican Irish woman.) Marx believed that, until the Irish were free from both British rule and racism, the English workers would not be able to free themselves, and the bourgeoisie could 'divide and rule'. He was equally aware of the oppression of India by British imperialism, and wrote against it in some of his *New York Tribune* articles. But he saw capitalism as the guilty party in these relations of oppression, and the proletariat as the only force strong enough to take on capitalism.

Likewise with the oppression of women. He doubtless shared the view of Engels, derived from Fourier (whom they had both studied) that the status of women in any society echoes the status of the working class in that society: it reflects slavery in slave societies, serfdom in feudal societies, and wage labour in capitalist societies. He clearly thought that the emancipation of the proletariat would emancipate women too.

In other words, insofar as Marx prioritized class, it was a causal priority based on explanatory theories about capitalist society, not a moral priority based on unconcern about some forms of oppression.

Morally, any case of oppression is equally bad; but if we want to understand all forms of oppression, and abolish them, we have to attend, first and foremost, to class.

Now it might be said, even if Marx was right 'that the emancipation of the class of producers involves all mankind, without distinction of race or sex' (as the head quote of this book states). He did not foresee another possibility: that the proletariat would not succeed in emancipating itself, but women and oppressed races would. And to some extent (but by no means entirely) that has happened. Certainly there has been a qualitative leap in the improvement of these groups' conditions, whereas the proletariat has only achieved quantitative improvements, consisting mainly of better wages, and has no more control over its conditions of existence than in Marx's time.

However, there is an asymmetry between the two sorts of liberation. The proletariat is constituted as the class that it is by its exploitation; it cannot emancipate itself without abolishing its status as proletariat and leaving no positions in society that benefit from exploitation. That is why the proletariat can never be fooled by that recent political opium, 'identity politics': it aims not at preserving its identity, but abolishing it. But sexes and races are defined independently of their oppression, and would continue to exist if emancipated. So if women or oppressed races are emancipated from their specific oppression without class exploitation being abolished, one effect would be that some women and members of erstwhile oppressed races would come to hold privileged positions in the still intact class hierarchy, and oppress their former sisters and brothers. This is largely what is meant by 'equality of opportunity'. And this aspect of emancipation (it is of course not the only one, but it is the main one that has happened) is of very doubtful value. Also, while class exploitation exists, it will always be profitable for the exploiters to find particular, vulnerable groups of workers that they can exploit even more severely than the rest, so the tendency to discrimination against some groups will remain.

Attempts by recent leftists to replace Marx's theory of classes by a generalized theory of oppression do not introduce any new moral issues that Marx had played down; but they do lose the specificity of his theory, its claim to not just describe and condemn but also to explain oppression in all its forms.

Now to the actual plans for political work that Marx derived from his theories. There are certain differences between those of his first involvement in practical politics (1847–52) and his later one (1864 on). In *The Communist Manifesto*, he sees tactics of communists as varying from country to country, depending on what other parties of the left exist. Where there is an independent mass-working-class party, like the Chartists in the United Kingdom, they join it and form its most conscious and internationalist element; where there are only petty bourgeois democratic parties, they give them varying degrees of support, while maintaining a separate working-class organization. In either case the political aim is to 'raise the proletariat to the position of ruling class, to win the battle of democracy' (*The Communist Manifesto*). These two clauses are seen as meaning the same, yet only in the United Kingdom would democracy (such as the Chartists proposed) have led to a working-class majority in parliament. Marx may have thought that in other countries the proletariat could come to power as head of an alliance of oppressed classes, proletariat, petty bourgeoisie and peasantry. However, he was aware that the petty bourgeoisie had their own parties, and both before and after the revolutions of 1848 urged the workers to organize themselves independently of those parties. During the upsurge of revolution in that year, he tended, as we have seen, to work for a broad democratic programme in alliance with bourgeois democrats, but as the revolutionary tide ebbed, he began to think that the initiative had to come from the proletariat. Thus in his address to the Communist League in March 1850 (already in exile in London) he mistakenly assumes that a new outbreak of democratic revolution will soon occur in Germany, and defends an independent proletarian party which, while it cannot yet take power, can push the petty bourgeoisie on to more extreme measures, including some nationalizations and taxation of the rich, while keeping its own proletarian organization and its own weapons (literally). This is seen as preparing the way for a workers' revolution. In this connection, Marx raises the slogan 'permanent revolution':

> It is our interest and our task to make the revolution permanent until all the more or less propertied classes have been driven from their

> ruling positions, until the proletariat has conquered state power. (*The Revolutions of 1848*, pp. 323–4)

This invites a whole lot of questions. What sort of timescale has Marx in mind? If the proletariat is to make its revolution against an already ruling petty bourgeoisie, it is hardly likely to have the support of that petty bourgeoisie, and in that case, must it not wait until it is the majority of the population, which presupposes a period, not of permanent revolution, but of peaceful economic expansion?

Moreover the measures that Marx thinks the proletariat can push the petty bourgeoisie into carrying out are largely the same measures as he proposes as the first measures of a proletarian revolutionary government: nationalization of land, transport, banks and large-scale production, heavy progressive taxation, arming of the people, and so on. It seems probable that Marx had not thought through this notion of permanent revolution, which makes its appearance in his works only briefly after the defeat of the German democratic revolution. It is, however, important historically, because it was taken up again by Trotsky in early twentieth-century Russia, at first rejected by Lenin, then, in 1917, adopted by him and, for a while, successfully carried out. The basis of the success, though, was the distribution of landed estates to the peasants, not their nationalization, as Marx advocated. Indeed, in Hungary in 1919 under the short-lived revolutionary socialist government of Bela Kun, the estates were nationalized instead of distributed, with the result that the peasants did not throw their weight behind the revolution, and it soon collapsed.

Anyway, Marx's brief 'permanent revolution' position is later referred to by Engels in these terms: if the French republic in 1848

> had concentrated the real power in the hands of the big bourgeoisie – monarchically inclined as it was – and on the other hand, had grouped all the other social classes, peasants as well as petty bourgeoisie, round the proletariat, so that, during and after the common victory, not they but the proletariat grown wise by experience must become the decisive factor – was there not every prospect here of turning the revolution of the minority into the revolution of the majority?
>
> History has proved us, and all who thought like us, wrong. It has made it clear that the state of economic development on the

Continent at that time was not, by a long way, ripe for the removal of capitalist production. ('Introduction to Class Struggles in France', *Selected Works in Two Volumes*, vol. 2, pp. 176–7)

Anyway, during his later period of political activity, Marx is far more concerned to build a well-organized mass working-class party which, during one of the recurrent economic crises that Marx argued were inherent in capitalism, could carry out a revolution with the clear support of the majority. Marx would no doubt have approved of Engels's metaphor of universal suffrage as a thermometer of class consciousness. When it shows boiling point, that is, when a working-class party wins a majority, then the struggle can be fought out under conditions most favourable to working-class victory. He certainly never made the mistake of thinking that an electoral victory by itself constituted a conquest of power. More of this in chapter seven, where I will also need to discuss the results of Marx's analysis of the Paris Commune. This analysis profoundly affects his notion of a workers' state, but it does not affect the issue of tactics, since the circumstances that brought about the Paris Commune were a unique combination of historical accidents. Doubtless that is true of any revolutionary situation, but the one thing that we can be sure of is that such combinations will never be twice alike.

Perhaps one more comment on Marx's view of the practice of party-programme writing will be in place. A consequence of Marx's rejection of utopianism is that the 'big' features of his programme must be left vague, to be specified according to the particular needs of the time and place. Thus it is clear that he advocates expropriating the capitalists by some form of common ownership. But whether this means nationalization (as *The Communist Manifesto* suggests for banks and transport), or municipalization, or internationalization, or turning over to workers' co-operatives (as happened to the workshops of absconding capitalists under the Paris Commune) is generally left for those who are there at the time to decide in view of their specific circumstances. However, on the details of political programmes, which of course are changed from election to election in accordance with the needs of the time, Marx is for great precision. After his theoretical *Critique of the Gotha Programme*, he objects to the vagueness of the specific measures demanded in the appendix: 'normal working day' – the length should be specified; 'prohibition of child labour' – the age limit should be given, and so on. This is a justified objection. Vagueness always makes it easier for politicians to break their promises to the electorate.

Labour, Value and Exploitation:
I. Theoretical

If Marx had been asked what he would be remembered by, he would undoubtedly have answered that it would be by the one lengthy book that he published in his lifetime, *Capital*, volume 1 – the only volume prepared by him for publication, and written while he was at the peak of his powers, and the volume, in my view, on which all the political conclusions rest (though some, such as Rosa Luxemburg, would disagree). Nevertheless, many of his other books are more popular today. This is partly due to *Capital*'s reputation for difficulty. It is true that the first nine of the thirty-three chapters are technical and abstract, though written in a crisp, clear style. But it is a technicality and abstractness required by the subject; Marx is not one of those thinkers who believes he has solved a problem whenever he has invented a new word. Nor does he go in for that kind of abstractness that is abstract because it is vague. He is scathing about that sort of abstractness, as in this passage:

> First of all, an abstraction is made from a fact; then it is declared that the fact is based on the abstraction. That is how to proceed if you want to appear German, profound and speculative.
>
> For example: Fact: The cat eats the mouse
> Reflection: Cat = nature, Mouse = nature; consumption of mouse by cat = consumption of nature by nature = self-consumption of nature.

Philosophic presentation of the fact: The devouring of the mouse by the cat is based upon the self-consumption of nature. (*The German Ideology*, ed. Pascal, pp. 114–15)

Indeed, anyone who takes the trouble to follow Marx's abstractions will also find that the text is not as dry as it is reputed to be. Its wit and irony often raise a chuckle.

Furthermore, many of the later chapters of *Capital* are full of historical and sociological description, which bring to life the plight of workers and peasants in his own time and during the rise of capitalism. Yet, without the abstract parts of the book, these descriptions would not show that the appalling conditions of those classes was an effect of the essential nature of capitalism. William Morris is credited, if apocryphally, with saying that he did not need Marx's *Capital* to tell him that the rich robbed the poor. Be that as it may, he read his copy of *Capital* (in French, since it had not yet been translated into English, and he was not fluent in German) until it fell apart and had to be rebound. And his own works show that he had assimilated its arguments well.

However, for those who find *Capital* too daunting, we are fortunate to have a brief account of its main concepts and arguments in the form of lectures given to English trade unionists belonging to the International, in a short work called *Value, Price and Profit* (or in some translations, *Wages, Price and Profit*). Wherever possible, I shall rely on this text in this chapter, though some reference to the larger work will be unavoidable.

It should also be mentioned that although Marx's main work is on economics, his reputation as a philosopher, a social theorist and a political thinker are all higher today than that as an economist. I think the reason for this is not that modern economics has refuted his ideas, but that it is about something different. It aims to predict economic events (without success, it may be said), whereas Marx was aiming to explain the structure of capitalism, its constraints and its developing tendencies.

What led Marx to write *Value, Price and Profit* was that one English member of the General Council of the International, 'Citizen Weston', as Marx calls him, was arguing that the wages of the entire working class were a fixed fund, so that if workers got a pay rise through their trade unions, they were doing so at the expense of their fellow workers, or if all workers got rises, these rises would be eroded by inflation and come to nothing. Although this 'wage fund theory' has now been discredited, it still makes its appearance in anti-trade-union journalism and political speeches. But Citizen Weston of course was not trying to hoodwink the workers into accepting their lot: on the contrary, he thought that only socialism would improve their condition, that trade-union activity under capitalism was pointless. Indeed Marx, before going on to refute Weston's position, praises his courage in putting forward a view so unpopular in the workers' movement. Nevertheless Marx (despite what is sometimes said about his supposed belief in 'increasing misery') argues that workers could, within limits, improve their lot within capitalism by trade-union action.

But in the process, Marx introduces us to some of his central distinctions: in particular between labour and labour-power; and he shows how exploitation can take place even when everything, including labour-power, is exchanged at its value.

In the first five chapters, Marx makes a factual rather than theoretical case against Weston, without introducing new technical terms. He points out that, firstly, it is a fact that the gross national product changes from year to year, and generally increases, and secondly, even if it did not, the proportion of wages to profits, within that magnitude, could change, and in fact does differ from country to country.

> The *will* of the capitalist is certainly to take as much as possible. What we have to do is not to talk about his *will*, but to inquire into his *power*, the *limits of that power*, and the *character of those limits*. (*Selected Works in One Volume*, p. 188)

(Elsewhere, Marx suggests that wages were high in America because land was cheap, and workers could therefore become small farmers, so they were not so trapped in the wage system as English workers.)

However, Weston thinks that wage rises will be passed on as price rises. But if the capitalist is already charging the highest price he can, how can he raise it? Only if the wage increase affects the market in some way. But how does the wage rise affect the market? If workers and capitalists were buying the same sort of goods, then a change in the proportion of the income that went to workers and to capitalists would not alter the amount of money chasing the same goods, and so would not affect prices. Suppose that the workers spend their money on necessities and the capitalists spend their profits on luxuries. Then if wages increase relative to profits, while supply remains constant, prices of necessities will rise, and the workers will only be able to buy what they did before; but Marx argues that, though this may happen in the short term, the capitalists producing luxuries (for which prices will have correspondingly lowered with the lower profits), will soon cotton on that there are higher profits to be made producing necessities, and part of the productive forces will switch to producing necessities. In due course, a new equilibrium will be reached, with a greater quantity of goods for workers' consumption.

Weston's assumption is: wages determine prices. It is assumed that profit is just a fixed proportion added to wages. But in that case, what determines wages? Why should the price of one commodity, 'labour', determine the price of all the others? And does it determine its own value? Weston seems to have got stuck in a circular argument where wages determine prices and prices determine wages. To get out of the circle we need to introduce some new concepts, which Marx does in chapters 6–9.

I shall look first at the distinction between use-value and exchange-value. Since in this text Marx is mainly talking about exchange-value, I shall draw on the early parts of *Capital* as well as *Value, Price and Profit*. I shall then look at the labour theory of value; then the distinction between labour and labour-power; and finally at the concept of exploitation. For the sake of exposition, it will be useful to think of exchange-value (or exchangeable value, as he calls it in this text), as meaning price. Actually it doesn't quite, as will be explained in the section on the labour theory of value. But it is the ratio in which two commodities exchange for each other, for example one pair of sandals = three bottles of rum; or in a money economy the ratio at which they tend to exchange for money. Hence the exchange-value of a commodity is measurable in money terms.

The use-value of a commodity is simply what it is useful for, for example, a pair of sandals is useful to wear, a bottle of rum is useful to get drunk on. It is the fact that different commodities have different use-values that makes them different commodities. No one would exchange a bottle of rum for another identical bottle of rum. Hence the idea fashionable a few years ago in postmodernist circles that under modern capitalism there are no use-values is nonsense. No use-values, no commodities. All that could be sensibly meant is that modern capitalism is exchange-value driven not use-value driven, but that is true of all capitalism, and so from the sixteenth century at least.

Use-value is a qualitative distinction, not a quantitative one, that is to say, the use-value of a commodity cannot be measured, it can only be described, and two commodities have use-values of different kinds (do you wear it or get drunk on it), not of different amounts. Of course, there can be a quantity of a particular use-value, like three bottles of rum, but one cannot quantify across different use-values. There is no answer to the question whether productivity is increased overall if more of one use-value and less of another is produced. One cannot ask whether one commodity has more use-value than another. Of course a temperance campaigner might say that sandals were more useful than rum, but that is a moral judgement, while the concept of a use-value is morally neutral. The use-value of an electric baton is to torture people, and it is therefore highly immoral that they are produced in England and sold to authoritarian regimes. But that is not the same as them having no use-value, which would simply mean that they could not become a commodity at all. On the other hand, things can have a use-value without being commodities, for instance air, or vegetables grown on the allotment for one's own use.

Now some economies are driven by the need to produce use-values, and some by the need to produce exchange-values. In a self-sufficient estate, for instance, whether a slave estate, a feudal estate, or a socialist commune, the decisions made about what is produced are determined by what use-values are needed – so much bread, so many raspberries, so much beer, and so on. In making decisions of what to produce one cannot calculate, for there is no common measure between the value of more bread and the value of more raspberries. If the estate is run rationally, the proportions will be decided by people's needs. Nothing can possibly be gained by producing more bread than the inhabitants can eat.

In capitalist society on the other hand, things are produced for sale. To a limited extent, this happens in a pre-capitalist craft community. A sandal-maker sells sandals in order to buy bread. But the exchange is still motivated by the use-value to be acquired at the end of it: you cannot eat sandals, you can eat bread. Marx distinguishes exchange of this form – commodity–money–commodity (C–M–C) – from the exchange in a market economy, which is money–commodity–money (M–C–M), that is, the merchant buys a commodity not in order to use it but in order to sell it. Since no one would go to this trouble to get the same amount of money as they had paid out in the first place, this always means money–commodity–more money. C–M–C exchange is motivated by the desire for a different use-value, M–C–M exchange by the desire for more money. Two whole different ways of life turn on this distinction. For a start, there is a limit to one's desires for use-values – when one has enough bread, more is not wanted. But in a money economy, more money is always wanted. This has effects on the intensity of exploitation. In a medieval village, the lord of the manor exploited the serfs. He ate a lot more than they did, but he only had one stomach, so there was a limit. There was therefore no point in his exploiting the serfs more than enough to get his supply of food. But if the village started producing for the world market, there would be no limit to how much he would try to get out of them, for it can all be cashed in money.

It is also significant that in most historical human societies, being use-value driven, unlimited desire for wealth is regarded as a vice, indeed an unnatural perversion of human nature. The Bible and Aristotle call it *pleonexia* (covetousness), and the European Middle Ages follow them. Buddhism and Taoism likewise condemn this vice. But in the capitalist world, it is regarded as a virtue. When villagers in a 'primitive', self-sufficient community are taught a more efficient way of producing their staple goods so they can do so in half the time, they may tend to work half as long and spend the rest of the time talking to their friends and neighbours. Western economists tend to regard this as 'irrational'. If they were 'rational' (read: covetous) they would spend all their spare time producing surplus goods and selling them, so they could buy TVs and would not need friends and neighbours any more.

Of course, both use-value driven and exchange-value driven societies can be exploitive. But there are nevertheless, for Marx, real advantages to use-value driven societies. This to some extent mitigates his general preference of capitalism to all pre-capitalist systems. Certainly, he sees socialism as a use-value driven system. This means that socialist economic planning could not be done by quantitative calculation. People would have to ask, 'What sort of world do we want to live in?' and plan production accordingly. You could not cost the value of a new motorway against the value of an ancient woodland; you would have to decide which you wanted. And any sort of maximization – of anything – would disappear.

In capitalist society, on the other hand, it is a matter of indifference as to what use-values are produced, and what use-values are destroyed in the process. Only quantity of exchange-value is considered. Herein is the source of all the irrationalities of capitalism, from the overproduction crises of Marx's time to the cutting down of the rainforest today.

Moreover, just as use-value driven economies generate one sort of ethical system, so exchange-value driven economies generate another, for which human desires are unlimited and moral reasoning is calculative. There are even economists today who try to explain friendship and marriage in terms of 'investment' for future profit to oneself. John Gay was satirizing early capitalism when he wrote the lines (in *The Beggar's Opera*):

> Friendship for interest is but a loan
> Each one pays out for what he can get.

Some modern economists elevate this into a principle, and even regard it as a truism. Such economists have abdicated the right to be considered human.

Marx's distinction between use-value and exchange-value, as we have seen, has far-reaching consequences. That is not true of the next idea to be looked at, the labour theory of value. Yet it is highly controversial. Part of the controversy is due to the fact that most modern economists reject this view. It is commonly regarded as something Marx just got wrong. I think it is more complex than that. Marx is trying to do something different from modern economists. For their purposes – advising capitalists on how to maximize profits or politicians on how to minimize welfare – their concept of price as determined by the equilibrium of supply and demand is quite adequate. For understanding how the economy as a whole constrains its parts, it is not. Marx was quite aware that prices at any given time were determined by the state of supply and demand; but he thought we should look for further explanations of why, for a particular product, supply and demand equilibriated at a particular price.

But there is another reason why Marx is so often attacked on this issue. It is widely believed that the labour theory of value entails that labour is the source of all wealth, and that therefore all wealth should belong to the workers – in other words that the labour theory of value by itself entails socialist conclusions. There is no truth in this. In the first place, this theory was not invented by Marx, but was common ground with such economists as Adam Smith and David Ricardo, who were strong advocates of capitalism. Secondly, when the authors of the German Social Democratic Party's Gotha Programme argued like this, Marx attacked them in the following terms:

> Labour is *not the source* of all wealth. *Nature* is just as much the source of use-values (and it is surely of such that material wealth consists!) as labour ... The bourgeois have very good grounds for falsely ascribing *supernatural creative power* to labour; since precisely from the fact that labour depends on nature it follows that the man who possesses no other property than his labour power must, in all conditions of society and culture, be the slave of other men who have made themselves the owners of the material conditions of labour. He can work only with their permission, hence live only with their permission. (*Selected Works in One Volume*, p. 319)

I remember reading these words in my study overlooking Snowdon one day and hearing almost simultaneously on the radio in another room, Margaret Thatcher, the then prime minister, making a speech telling people to 'go out and create wealth' – something that over four million of our compatriots could not do since, as a result of her policies, they were unemployed.

Thirdly, neo-Marxist economists have had no trouble reformulating Marx's theory of exploitation so that it is independent of the labour theory of value.

Still, Marx did hold the labour theory of value, so we should find out what he meant by it. Value is seen as identical with price only at equilibrium. ('Value' here is connected with exchange-value rather than use-value, but Marx uses 'value' without a prefix to denote the social essence of value, 'exchange-value' to denote the form in which it appears in the market.) Supply and demand determine the price, which fluctuates around the value, and tends towards it. Value-theory is seen as explaining why supply and demand equilibriate where they do.

Value in this sense is said to be determined by the amount of labour incorporated in a commodity, that is, the labour it takes (on average in a given society) to produce it. In the case of a woollen coat for instance, this includes the shepherd's labour raising sheep, the shearer's labour shearing them, the transporter's labour taking the wool to be made into yarn, the spinner's and weaver's and tailor's labour, the labour of the engineers who made the loom, and so on. If it takes twice as much labour to make a coat as to make a pair of sandals, the value of the coat will be twice that of the sandals.

Why did Marx believe this? In *Value, Price and Profit* he gives only a sketch of a reason, namely:

> As the *exchangeable values* of commodities are only *social functions* of those things, and have nothing at all to do with their *natural* qualities, we must first ask, What is the common *social substance* of all commodities? It is *Labour*. (*Selected Works in One Volume*, p. 203)

I think we need to look at a passage in *Capital* to fill this out. It approaches the question by looking first at the whole of a society's production, a quantity of a given commodity being a proportion of this product, expressing some fraction of the total social labour time. Marx illustrates this by looking at three non-capitalist 'societies' (in one case a society of one), in which the relation of products to each other as products of fractions of the total social labour is transparent.

Since Robinson Crusoe's experiences are a favourite theme with political economists, let us take a look at him on his island ... In spite of the variety of his work, he knows that his labour, whatever its form, is but the activity of one and the same Robinson, and consequently, that it consists of nothing but different modes of human labour. Necessity itself compels him to apportion his time accurately between his different kinds of work. Whether one kind occupies a greater space in his general activity than another, depends on the difficulties, greater or less as the case may be, to be overcome in attaining the useful effect aimed at. This our friend Robinson soon learns by experience, and having rescued a watch, ledger, pen and ink from the wreck, commences, like a true-born Briton, to keep a set of books. His stock-book contains a list of the objects of utility that belong to him, of the operations necessary for their production; and lastly, of the labour-time that definite quantities of those objects have, on average, cost him. All the relations between Robinson and the objects that form this wealth of his own creation, are here so simple and clear as to be intelligible without exertion, even to Mr Sedley Taylor. And yet those relations contain all that is essential to the determination of value. (*Capital*, vol. 1, 1959, pp. 76–7*)

(Mr Sedley Taylor, who is not mentioned elsewhere in *Capital*, was a Cambridge man who later accused Marx, it seems without foundation, of misreporting a budget speech of Gladstone's. Here he appears simply as an example of a none-too-intelligent intellectual.) Marx gives us two more examples, first of a medieval village, and then virtually the only paragraph in *Capital* that describes a socialist community:

Let us now picture to ourselves, by way of a change, a community of free individuals, carrying on their work with the means of production in common, in which the labour-power of all the different individuals is consciously applied as the combined labour-power of the community. All the characteristics of Robinson's labour are repeated, but with this difference, that they are social, instead of individual. Everything produced by him was exclusively the result of his own personal labour, and therefore simply an object of use for himself. The total labour of our community is a social product. One

---

* In this chapter and the next I use the Moore/Aveling translation of *Capital*, since it gives more of the authentic flavour of Marx's time.

portion serves as fresh means of production and remains social. But another portion is consumed by the members as means of subsistence. (p. 78)

So society, when united either in one individual or one community governing its own economic life, 'exchanges' units of one commodity for those of another only by apportioning a greater proportion of the total social labour from one commodity to another. Ultimately, this is what must happen in a market economy too. But the apportioning is not done by individual or collective decision, but by the constraints of the market. Hence, while it is natural to express exchange-value in money terms, its essence, value, is strictly expressed as a fraction: a unit of a commodity represents a given fraction of the total social labour, and exchanges with units of other commodities that represent the same fraction. Thus there can be no concept of growth in value terms, since the total value produced by a community is the sum of all its fractions, which by definition = 1. There can of course be growth in use-value terms and, given humankind's tendency to advance technologically, there usually is. But since this spans qualitatively different use-values, it cannot be measured by a common measure.

Now we come to the second pair of concepts distinguished by Marx: labour and labour-power. Once again, a lot of misconceptions have arisen about this. On the one hand, it is sometimes assumed that labour-power are just Marx's words for labour. I have seen a popular philosophy textbook where it is said that Marx taught that labour-power is the source of value. This would not even be meaningful according to Marx's definitions: it is *labour* that creates value. On the other hand, some people seem to think that there is something mysterious and even elevated about the concept of labour-power. Not so. It would be much better to be the owner of labour rather than merely the owner of labour-power.

I think the over-literal translation of the German in *Capital* is partly to blame. In *Value, Price and Profit* the phrase is rendered as 'labouring power', which is better English and less likely to be misunderstood. Marx's essential point is that it is incorrect to talk about the buying and selling of labour, wages as the price of labour, and so on. (Though Marx sometimes does so as shorthand, meaning price of labour-power, and so on.) What is sold by the worker and bought by the capitalist is not labour but labour-power. Why? Well, the proletarian cannot sell labour because it is not in his or her possession to sell. In order to labour, one has to have means of labour – a workplace, tools, raw materials, and so on. These the proletarian does not have, and so cannot labour. What he or she does have is the capacity or power to labour, which can only be exercised if he or she acquires access to the means of labour. In order to acquire that access, and to labour, the worker must sell his or her power of labouring to a capitalist. When I studied economics at school, we were taught that there were three 'factors of production', namely 'land' (that is, nature), 'labour' and 'capital' (that is, manufactured means of labour). Each was supposed to be a distinct contribution to the production process, and receive a just return as rent, wages and profits. But of course 'when Adam delved and Eve span', the labour process included the spade and the soil, the spinning wheel and the wool; these did not have a separate supplier or yield a separable return. As Marx asks:

> How does this strange phenomenon arise, that we find on the market a set of buyers, possessed of land, machinery, raw material, and the means of subsistence, all of them, save land in its crude state, the *products of labour*, and on the other hand, a set of sellers who have nothing to sell except their labouring power, their working arms and brains? That the one set buys continually in order to make a profit and enrich themselves, while the other set continually sells in order to earn their livelihood? The inquiry into this question would be an inquiry into what the economists call '*Previous, or Original Accumulation*', but which ought to be called *Original Expropriation*. We should find that this so-called *Original Accumulation* means nothing but a series of historical processes, resulting in a *Decomposition of the Original Union* existing between the Labouring Man and his Instruments of Labour. Such an inquiry, however, lies beyond the pale of my present subject. [See next chapter.] The *Separation* between the man of Labour and the Instruments of Labour once established, such a state of things will maintain itself and reproduce itself upon a constantly increasing scale, until a new and fundamental revolution in the mode of production should again overturn it, and restore the original union in a new historical form. (*Selected Works in One Volume*, p. 210)

I have said that the labour theory of value is a bland theory without political entailments. This is not true of the distinction between labour and labour-power: it is pregnant with revolutionary implications, for it is a distinction made real by the 'decomposition' of an original unity of labour into labour-power and the means of labour – a decomposition effected by a historical act of expropriating workers, as we shall see in the next chapter. It is this expropriation that compels workers to come back, cap in hand, to ask for access to what is proper to their trade, and hence properly theirs.

If labour is the measure of value, does it make any sense to talk about the 'value of labour'? We can of course talk about the value created by, say, eight hours of labour: it is eight hours' worth. But this is mere tautology. What the worker sells to the employer is his or her labour-power, that is, their capacity to work for a given period of time. The employer then unites that labour-power with specific means of production and raw materials, and sets it to work. The result is labour. The labour adds, say, eight hours' worth of value to the raw materials in working on them. But what the worker has been paid for is not eight hours' labour but eight hours' labour-power. The labour creates a value, but it does not have a measurable value. The labour-power has a measurable value, which is not connected with the value created by the labour.

Thus Marx escapes Weston's circle: for Weston, the price of labour determines the price of commodities which determines the price of labour. For Marx, the labour-power has a value = v; the labour-power is put to work as labour, which creates value = v + surplus. While the value of eight hours' labour-power will not rise above the value added to the commodities in eight hours' labour (the employer would not buy labour-power at such a price), the value of labour-power and the value it creates when put to work as labour are in other respects independent variables.

This brings us to the concept of exploitation. It is labour that adds value to commodities, and eight hours of labour adds eight hours' worth of value. But it is labour-power that has a value and can be exchanged at it. The value of eight hours of labour-power is not determined by the value eight hours of labour will produce, but by the amount of labour needed to produce *it*. This may sound odd at first. How much labour is needed to produce eight hours of labour-power? The answer is: enough labour to produce what the worker needs in order to live, and be fit enough to do eight hours' labour. But in any economy more advanced than a primitive subsistence economy, less than eight hours' labour will suffice for that. For the sake of argument, let us assume that four hours' labour will produce eight hours' labour-power (the working day being eight hours and four hours being enough to produce what the worker needs to live on for a day). So the worker will be paid for the produce of four hours of labour when he has done eight. In a feudal village, this is obvious: the serf works half the time on his own land and half, without payment, on the lord of the manor's land. The rate of exploitation is visible in the different fields that the serf is working in on different days. But with the proletarian it is different: the rate of exploitation is obscured, because, while the worker is paid half what their labour produces, they are paid the whole value of their labour-power. Hence exploitation takes place when everything, including labour-power, is exchanged at its value.

Exploitation, then, is not some kind of cheating whereby particularly nasty capitalists pay less than the value for labour-power. Such capitalists exist, but the system would still be exploitive without them. Even if all capitalists paid a little more than its value for labour-power, they would still be exploiting the workers, because what they paid would be less than the labour produced. The rate of exploitation is the ratio between the value of labour-power, and the value that the labour will produce when that labour-power is put to work. It is an objective ratio, and is, at least approximately, measurable. Marx calls the surplus produced by labour over what is paid for the labour-power 'surplus value'. This is his more technical term for exploitation, and rent, interest and profit all form part of surplus value.

Some commentators have complained that by using the term 'exploitation' Marx is introducing a condemning value-judgement into what is supposed to be a scientific account. But the term is defined quite precisely. It acquires its negative value-judgement, not in addition to what it means, but because of what it means. Indeed, talking as he was to English trade unionists, Marx introduces the word 'exploitation' with the apology: 'you must allow me this French word'. Presumably it was not yet in common use in England, so can hardly have been chosen for its ready-made evaluative connotations. Indeed both its common use and its value-ladenness may be largely due to the influence of Marx and the definition he gave the word.

Now if the value of labour-power is determined by subsistence, does that not put us back where we started, with Weston's iron law of wages? If subsistence were defined purely by physical survival, this would be true: wages could never rise above this minimum. But as we have seen, while they cannot for long, or everywhere fall below this minimum (though they have for a while in some places where labour-power was available from outside to replace local workers who had been killed by overwork and undernourishment), they can and usually do rise above this minimum. The tendency of the capitalist is to reduce wages to this minimum, and increase working hours to their physical maximum, because that will maximize surplus value. But in the first place, workers by combining in unions can force the price up, and by bringing pressure to bear on governments to legislate, can limit working hours. Does this mean that the price of labour-power rises above its value? No, because

> The value of the labouring power is formed by two elements – the one merely physical, the other historical or social ... Besides this mere physical element, the value of labour is in every country determined by a *traditional standard of life*. It is not mere physical life, but it is the satisfaction of certain wants springing from the social conditions in which people are placed and reared up. (*Selected Works in One Volume*, p. 225)

The traditional standard of living in one country may be higher than in another, or may be expressed in different use-values. Marx says somewhere that French workers need wine while English workers need beer. By itself this explanation by custom seems as unsatisfactory as explanation in terms of the will of the capitalists being different in the UK and the USA. But if we combine it with an account in terms of the bargaining power of classes, it is more fruitful. If American workers became the highest paid in the world in the nineteenth century because land was cheap, they then refused to accept lower wages even when the supply of land was exhausted, and are still the highest paid in the world. It is the long-term balance of power between the classes that determines the customary level of 'subsistence'. Of course, within a capitalist society, the capitalists are always more powerful than the workers, but not infinitely more. In the UK, from Attlee's government in the 1940s through to Wilson's in the 1970s, the workers were relatively powerful, even under conservative governments. Since Thatcher, they have been much less so, even under Labour governments. As a result, workers will now accept conditions they would not have considered when I first went to work in 1962. Thatcher has made us into a nation of crawlers.

It should be noted that Marx's account shows not only how wages and surplus value are produced, but how the relations of production that produce them – the separation of the means of labour from the worker and their monopolization by capitalists – are reproduced from generation to generation. The worker produces not only his or her own means of survival as a supplier of labour-power, but also the new means of labour with which the capitalist will employ their sons and daughters.

Labour, Value and Exploitation: II. Historical

In addition to the theoretical input into Marx's main work, there was a considerable input from factual knowledge both of the history of English capitalism and contemporary English factory conditions. Marx explains in his preface the reason for taking his historical material from England:

> The physicist either observes physical phenomena where they occur in their most typical form and most free from disturbing influence, or, wherever possible, he makes experiments under conditions that assure the occurrence of the phenomenon in its normality. In this work I have to examine the capitalist mode of production, and the conditions of production and exchange corresponding to that mode. Up to the present time, their classic ground is England. That is the reason why England is used as the chief illustration in the development of my theoretical ideas. (*Capital*, 1959, p. 8)

Marx goes on to tell his German readers that this is also their future, and indeed that where industry had already developed in Germany, the situation was far worse for lack of factory legislation. He also praises the English factory inspectors very highly:

> We should be appalled by the state of things at home if, as in England, our governments and parliaments appointed periodically commissions of inquiry into economic conditions;

85

if these commissions were armed with the same plenary powers to get at the truth; if it was possible to find for this purpose men as competent, as free from partisanship and respect of persons as are the English factory-inspectors, her medical reporters on public health, her commissioners of inquiry into the exploitation of women and children, into housing and food. (p. 9)

Marx himself read the reports of these inspectors with great care, and they are often quoted in *Capital*.

I want in this chapter to look at two very different sections in *Capital* which show this work in its factual dimension. The first is one of the parts where Marx shows what exploitation meant in real terms to the workers who suffered it, the chapter on the working day. The second is an account of how, in historical fact, the separation of the means of labour from the worker came about.

The working day

In the first section of the chapter on the working day, Marx sets up a hypothetical debate between the capitalist as the personification of self-expanding capital, and a worker. The worker's case is apparently along the lines of a real manifesto issued by London builders striking for a nine-hour day. The capitalist, having bought a day's labour-power, wants the worker to work as many hours in that day as is possible, resting only enough to be back on the job the next morning. For the price of a day's labour-power is to maintain the worker for a day, and the more hours worked in that day the more the surplus that accrues to the capitalist. It is in this connection that Marx uses a metaphor very reminiscent of his early writing. Calling capital 'dead labour' (since the means of labour that are the material embodiment of capital are the product of past labour), Marx writes that, 'Capital is dead labour, that, vampire-like, only lives by sucking living labour, and lives the more, the more labour it sucks' (p. 233).

The worker, on the other hand, puts another gloss on the question of what the capitalist has legitimately bought. Suppose, he says, that overwork kills him in ten years, when he could otherwise have expected a working life of thirty years: the capitalist is using up three days' labour-power for the price of one.

Of course, from a human point of view, the worker ought to be able to live out his natural life, but from the point of view of the law of exchanges, capitalist and worker have equal claims here.

> Between equal rights force decides. Hence it is that in the history of capitalist production, the determination of what is a working day, presents itself as the result of a struggle, a struggle between collective capital, i.e. the class of capitalists, and collective labour, i.e. the working class. (p. 235)

In the second section of this chapter, Marx compares capitalist exploitation with exploitation in pre-capitalist societies. He mentions that:

> Where not the exchange-value but the use-value of the product predominates, surplus-labour will be limited by a given set of wants which may be greater or less, and that here no boundless thirst for surplus-labour arises from the nature of the production itself. Hence in antiquity overwork becomes horrible only when the object is to obtain exchange-value in its specific independent money form; in the production of gold and silver. (p. 235)

He quotes Diodorous Siculus on working to death in the ancient gold mines. The Athenian silver mines at Lavrion would be another example.

Marx goes on to compare the neo-feudal exploitation of peasants in nineteenth-century Romania with the exploitation of proletarians in England. In both cases, production is for the market, so there is an unlimited demand for surplus labour; but in Romania, surplus labour took the 'visible' form or a corvée or conscription of peasants' labour to work for the boyards (aristocrats) on a certain number of days per year. Marx points out that, just as English manufacturers did, the boyards strove, legally or illegally, to maximize the hours of peasants' labour that they could conscript.

Section three of the chapter on the working day has the title 'Branches of English Industry without Legal Limits to Exploitation'. Just as a chemist will ensure that the materials used in their experiments are pure, and a student of animal behaviour will observe animals in conditions unaffected by interaction with humans by concealing cameras in their habitats, so Marx, in order to study capitalism in its pure or 'wild' form, looks at industries unaffected by legislation. This will establish *tendencies* inherent in capitalism, which tendencies are in modern societies modified by political restraints, but still exist, just as gravity is operating even when the roof is not falling on your head. Much of this chapter is quoted from reports of magistrates, doctors or other concerned authorities.

Factory legislation had initially been restricted to the textile industry. Marx's first example of unlimited exploitation is the lace industry, where children of nine or ten worked from two, three or four in the morning till ten, eleven or twelve at night. This is asserted by a magistrate at a meeting in Nottingham in 1860, and reported in the *Daily Telegraph* from which Marx quotes it. The magistrate refers to:

> Their limbs wearing away, their frames dwindling, their faces whitening, and their humanity absolutely sinking into a stone-like torpor, utterly horrible to contemplate ... We are not surprised that Mr Mallett, or any other manufacturer, should stand forward and protest against discussion ... The system, as the Rev. Montagu Valpy describes it, is one of unmitigated slavery, socially, physically, morally, and spiritually. (pp. 243–4)

Marx next discusses the pottery industry, in which children of seven were worked fifteen hours a day. Statistics also showed that adult workers in this industry were being killed by their work: in Stoke-on-Trent, 36.6 per cent of the population were potters, but more than half the deaths were from lung diseases caused by working in pottery. Only immigration from rural areas kept the population going.

Although the length of the working day is Marx's main concern in this chapter, working conditions are discussed insofar as they ruin health and shorten workers' lives. In the manufacture of Lucifer matches, a kind of lockjaw was caused by chemical pollution. There was

> a range of the working day from 12 to 14 or 15 hours, night-labour, irregular meal times, meals for the most part taken in the very work-rooms that are pestilent with phosphorus. Dante would have found the worst horrors of his Inferno surpassed in this manufacture. (p. 246)

Children as young as six were among those working in these conditions.

Marx also documents the dangers to the public of overwork in transport industries. Railway employees prosecuted after an accident that had killed hundreds pointed out that their working day had, over the last five or six years, been raised from eight hours to fourteen, eighteen or twenty hours.

After a discussion of nightwork – and adulteration of goods – in baking, Marx concludes this section with an account of a woman who was literally worked to death in a fashionable London milliners, and of the degeneration under capitalism of conditions in the blacksmith's trade, once regarded as a healthy occupation in its rural setting, but which had been so changed by the unlimited demands of capitalist exploitation that it was dramatically shortening the lives of its workers. The blacksmith

> can strike so many blows per day, walk so many steps, breathe so many breaths, produce so much work, and live an average, say, of fifty years; he is made to strike so many more blows, to walk so many more steps, to breathe so many more breaths per day, and to increase altogether a fourth of his life. He meets the effort; the result is, that producing for a limited time a fourth more work, he dies at 37 for 50. (p. 256)

Of course, the tendency of capitalism documented in this chapter – the tendency to extend the working day to its physical maximum – has since been offset in every trade (in prosperous countries) by legislation and trade-union action. But as a tendency it still exists, and occasionally is illegally realized. The same is rather more often true of unhealthy working conditions. A friend of mine who worked in motor manufacture was told by his doctor to give up his job if he valued his lungs. And in jobs that are not paid an hourly rate, unpaid overtime is often enforced.

In the following section, Marx discusses nightwork and the relay system, whereby (for instance) steelworks were kept open at all hours, exploiting child labour at night as well as day. This may be the place for a word about Marx's attitude to women's labour, which he mentions here. He certainly saw the involvement of women in productive industrial work as something that had come to stay and which, under conditions more suitable to human beings, would be liberating. He had no wish to limit women to domestic labour. Indeed, even child labour had his support provided it was in healthy conditions, and combined with education. But he just as certainly thought that some trades were unsuitable for women. In this section, he says, 'In some branches of industry, the girls and women work through the night together with the males' (p. 257) and he appends in a footnote a quote from an inspector's report:

> These females employed with the men, hardly distinguished from them in their dress, and begrimed with dirt and smoke, are exposed to the deterioration of character, arising from the loss of self-respect, which can hardly fail to follow from their unfeminine occupation.

Marx clearly approves of these comments and concludes that women should not be employed in this kind of work. If anyone feels that this makes him a collaborator in the oppression of women, it should be said in his defence that the women of that period were only too glad to get out of trades of this nature, and did not see this as a restriction of their 'freedom of labour', any more than did the men who were effectively prevented from working more than ten hours by the factory acts (though the employers tried to depict the factory acts as such a restriction on freedom).

In section five, Marx looks at the pre-history of the struggle to reduce the working day. He again points out that the capitalist wants the whole twenty-four hours, minus only what is necessary to enable the worker to get back to work next day, and does not have any regard for

> time for education, for intellectual development, for the fulfilling of social functions and for social intercourse, for the free play of his bodily and mental activity, even the rest time of Sunday (and that in a country of Sabbatarians!) – moonshine! (p. 264)

He mentions that rural workers were still sometimes imprisoned for working in the garden on a Sunday, yet a factory worker would be punished for breach of contract if he failed to work for his boss on a Sunday, even if his motives were religious.

For Marx, the issue at stake is whether the worker is 'nothing else, his whole life through, than labour-power' or whether he or she also had a life to live. But the capitalist goes even further than just reducing the worker to labour-power.

> But in its blind, unrestrainable passion, its werewolf hunger for surplus-labour, capital oversteps not only the moral, but even the merely physical maximum bounds of the working day. It usurps the time for growth, development and healthy maintenance of the body. (pp. 264–5)

In this connection, Marx compares wage labour in the UK with slavery in the USA. As long as slaves were irreplaceable workers on an isolated estate, the master had some self-interest in keeping them alive and well. But since it became possible to work your slave to death in Georgia or Mississippi and replace them with new slaves from Kentucky or Virginia, this was what many masters did. But this was parallel with what happened in some of the industrial towns of England and Scotland, as has already been mentioned in connection with the potteries. Proletarians who had been worked into an early grave were replaced by workers emigrating from rural districts, or from Ireland. Marx quotes from a speech in the House of Commons in 1863:

> The cotton trade has existed for ninety years ... It has existed for three generations of the English race, and I believe I may safely say that during that period it has destroyed nine generations of factory operatives. (p. 267)

Marx shows in this section that the individual capitalist is not necessarily to blame, but rather the system, for 'Free competition brings out the inherent laws of capitalist production, in the shape of external coercive laws having power over every individual capitalist' (p. 270). He mentions that twenty-six firms in the potteries, including Wedgwood, petitioned for legislation limiting working hours for children, since without such legislation no capitalist was free to introduce decent conditions, as the competition of those who did not would drive them out of business.

Free competition between capitalists does not unambiguously mean freedom, even for capitalists; capitalists may not be free to treat their workers decently unless they – and their competitors – are *compelled* to treat their workers decently. This shows why Marx should be taken seriously when he writes in the preface to *Capital*:

> To prevent possible misunderstanding, a word. I paint the capitalist and the landlord in no sense *couleur de rose*. But here individuals are dealt with only in so far as they are the personifications of economic categories, embodiments of particular class-relations and class-interests. My standpoint, from which the evolution of the economic formation of society is viewed as a process of natural history, can less than any other make the individual responsible for relations whose creature he socially remains, however much he may subjectively raise himself above them. (p. 10)

So Marx is in no sense a 'lifestyle socialist': he does not think that being a socialist entails trying to live as if socialism already existed, or trying to refuse to participate in capitalist institutions and practices, both of which are impossible. Being a socialist in a capitalist society means working for socialism, no more and no less.

Marx goes on to discuss the history of legislation about the working day. In his own time, such legislation was aimed at limiting the working day; but from the late Middle Ages till shortly before Marx's time, legislation about the working day aimed to increase it. This makes it look as though there had been progress by Marx's time, and in a sense there had. But working hours in Marx's time were, in absolute terms, longer than in the pre-capitalist period when governments had been trying to lengthen them.

Thus the statute of 1496, in Henry Tudor's time, set summer working hours (winter hours would have been shorter) as five a.m. till seven or eight p.m., with a total of three hours for meal breaks. This adds up to eleven or twelve hours, which is shorter than was commonly worked in the early nineteenth century, before the factory acts. Moreover, while capitalists in Marx's time often broke the law and worked their labourers for longer hours, in King Henry's time the opposite happened – hours were in practice shorter than the law required. Thus the working day had in practice increased with the coming of industrial capitalism. Marx quotes the recent law in Massachusetts which limited child labour to twelve hours a day, and comments that in the mid-seventeenth century this was the normal working day for able-bodied adults.

Marx quotes at length an eighteenth-century debate over whether it was desirable to compel workers to work a six-day week. Postlethwaite urges that the ingenuity and dexterity of English handworkers derives from their having leisure to relax in their own way. The author of an 'Essay on Trade and Commerce' disagrees, and recommends workhouses, which are 'houses of terror', with a twelve-hour working day, to intimidate workers into accepting longer hours with lower pay. Yet this twelve-hour day was, by the 1830s, regarded as dangerously short by the advocates of *laissez-faire*, when it was enacted for children of thirteen to eighteen. Likewise in France, the twelve-hour day was enacted during the Second Republic, and defended as the one good thing remaining from the Republic when Louis Bonaparte (Napoleon III) sought to tamper with it.

This all indicates that capitalism had in fact increased the working day, where pre-capitalist and early capitalist legislation had failed to do so.

Marx goes on in section six to discuss the factory acts in the United Kingdom, which he sees as victories in the workers' struggle, resisted and often disobeyed by most of the capitalists.

The first step was the 1833 Act, which set the working day at twelve hours for thirteen- to eighteen-year-olds, and eight hours for children of nine to thirteen. Marx argues that it was not properly enforced until 1844, when it was extended to women, and effectively to men, since bosses could not work the factory profitably without female and child labour. In 1847 the working day was reduced to ten hours. Capitalists responded by reducing wages by twenty-five per cent, and organizing petitions against the act, which some workers signed under duress. Marx quotes from a report of the factory inspectors the following dialogue and comment:

> 'Though I signed it [the petition], I said at the time I was putting my hand to a wrong thing.' 'Then why did you put your hand to it?' 'Because I should have been turned off if I had refused.' Whence it would appear that this petitioner felt himself 'oppressed', but not exactly by the Factory Act. (p. 284 n. 3)

Some capitalists also retaliated by sacking women and young people and reintroducing nightwork for men. Others avoided giving the statutory meal breaks by saying that the meal times were before work started in the morning and after it finished in the evening.

Nevertheless, the factory acts came to be accepted by society at large, and later, in the 1860s, were extended to industries other than textiles.

> It will be easily understood that after the factory magnates had resigned themselves and become reconciled to the inevitable, the power of resistance of capital gradually weakened, whilst at the same time the power of attack of the working class grew with the number of its allies in the classes of society not immediately interested in the question. Hence the comparatively rapid advance since 1860. (p. 296)

In section seven, Marx looks at the spread of factory legislation to other countries. After the 1848 revolution, French workers got a twelve-hour day, explicitly for all, not just women and children, while

> In the United States of North America, every independent movement of the workers was paralysed so long as slavery disfigured a part of the Republic. Labour cannot emancipate itself in the white skin where in the black it is branded. But out of the death of slavery a new life at once arose. The first fruit of the Civil War was the eight hours' agitation, that ran with the seven-leagued boots of the locomotive from the Atlantic to the Pacific, from New England to California. (p. 301)

The eight-hour day also became one of the aims of the First International.

Marx sees the whole history of the working day as a prolonged class struggle. It was waged in various ways: by legislation, by campaigning on both sides for legislation, by industrial actions of various sorts on both sides, and by law-breaking on both sides. The law for Marx can always be seen as a weapon in class struggle, and if it is one side's weapon, the other side will break it if possible and necessary. Class struggle has often taken the form of law-breaking: by oppressors, from Henry III breaking the Magna Carta, to modern bosses paying below the minimum wage; and by the oppressed, from

Robin Hood and his merry men, to modern strikers breaking Thatcher's anti-union legislation.

In *Capital*, the question of the working day has become central to Marx's thought. The concept of exploitation involves the idea that only part of the working day is for the worker's benefit, the remainder producing the boss's unearned surplus. And the idea of having free time has become central to Marx's notion of a society in which human fulfilment is possible. Thus he says in volume III of *Capital*:

> Just as the savage must wrestle with Nature to satisfy his wants, to maintain and reproduce life, so must civilized man, and he must do so in all social formations and under all possible modes of production. With his development this realm of necessity expands as a result of his wants; but, at the same time, the forces of production which satisfy these wants also increase. Freedom in this field can only consist in socialized man, the associated producers, rationally regulating their interchange with Nature, bringing it under their common control, instead of being ruled by it as by the blind forces of Nature; and achieving this with the least expenditure of energy and under conditions most favourable to, and worthy of, their human nature. But it nonetheless still remains a realm of necessity. Beyond it begins that development of human energy which is an end in itself, the true realm of freedom, which, however, can blossom forth only with this realm of necessity as its basis. The shortening of the working day is its basic prerequisite. (pp. 799–800)

Commentators have noted that reading *Capital* often leaves the reader with an intense hatred of capitalism, and no doubt this was Marx's intention. The hatred is aroused mostly by perfectly objective reporting of the evils perpetrated by capitalism when it was untrammelled by legislation and trade-union resistance. But of course in all long-industrialized countries, capitalism is now subjected to those limits. Taken by themselves, the horrific histories recounted in *Capital* could be an argument for those limits, rather than for abolishing capitalism altogether. But at least it should be recognized that the tendency of capitalism is to transgress those limits; that even today it is engaged in constant struggle to loosen the restraints of legislation and to weaken the trade unions. It is a constant struggle on the part of the working class to keep the limits in place. Furthermore, modern capitalism can often avoid them altogether by transferring its investment to countries where the restraints are weak or non-existent. And it has succeeded in creating a new 'long hours' culture, where many fathers only see their children awake on Sundays, and people who want to leave work after an eight-hour day are caricatured as dinosaurs. Throughout the nineteenth century and the first two decades of the twentieth, working hours were reduced, but then something of a plateau was reached, and in the United Kingdom since Thatcher they have risen again. It is perhaps timely to return to Marx's programme for shortening the working day as the prerequisite of a 'realm of freedom' for humankind.

For those who find mathematical economics congenial, there is a section in *Capital* just before the chapter on the working day (pp. 224–9), called 'Senior's "Last Hour"'. Here Marx takes to task the capitalist economist Nassau Senior, who calculated, just before the Ten Hours Act was passed, that all the profit in the textile industry was made in the last hour of the eleven-and-a-half-hour working day, and hence would disappear if the act were passed. Marx argues that Senior has miscalculated by assuming that the greater part of the working day was devoted, not to producing either wages or profit, but to replacing the capital laid out by the capitalist on plant and machinery. Marx's own calculation based on Senior's figures gives half the working day each to the production of wages and profits, and therefore predicts that the ten-hour day would still allow a substantial profit, eighty-two per cent instead of the one-hundred per cent prior to the Ten Hours Act. The capital laid out is not replaced by new value-creation, but its value is transferred to the product in proportion as it is used up. The outcome of the Ten Hours Act, which did not ruin industry, confirmed Marx's predictions.

Primitive accumulation

Marx has explained how the decomposition of production into capital and labour-power reproduces itself from year to year and from generation to generation, so that whatever any individual does, relations of exploitation survive. He has also made it clear that this decomposition is not given by nature – it is a historical fact that the worker under capitalism has been deprived of his or her means of labour. But how did this fact come about historically?

Apologists of capitalism have given an account that makes it look as if, whatever we think of capitalism now, its origins are just. And there are still political philosophers today who think that a just distribution is one that has come about by free contracts from a just starting point. This is the view of Robert Nozick and his followers. The classical account goes like this: originally all were equal, but some worked hard and saved what they earned, while others were lazy or spendthrift; the former came to own capital, the latter not, and the latter, or their descendants, ended up as propertiless proletarians working for the former.

Actually it is not at all clear that this is even coherent. In a non-money economy, one could not accumulate capital; if you worked harder than your neighbour and produced more meat and vegetables, you might have a bigger Christmas dinner, but you could not keep them long. Saving presupposes money, and money presupposes that people already have power over the labour of others, for that is just what money is. However, Marx is not here concerned to prove that this 'just' primitive accumulation could not have taken place, but simply that it did not.

The process by which a class of proletarians without the means of labour came to exist alongside a class of capitalists with those means was very different. In the first place, though individual production did exist in the pre-capitalist world, there was not an economy of independent equals; the starting point of the process was another class society: feudalism. When serfs became legally free, in late-medieval England for example, they did not become equals with their lords, but tenants or, in some cases, wage labourers, most of whom would have had a few acres of land to farm on their own account. They may have had more independence than a proletarian, but they were a relatively underprivileged class, and were exploited through rent and interest.

Marx's main concern, though, is with the next stage in the history: the way free peasants and artisans of the late Middle Ages were transformed into wage labourers. This started to happen in England first of all in the Tudor period.

> In insolent conflict with king and parliament, the great feudal lords created an incomparably larger proletariat by the forcible driving of the peasantry from the land, to which the latter had the same feudal rights as the lord himself, and by the usurpation of the common lands. (*Capital*, vol. I, p. 718)

The motive for this was the growth of the wool trade. Peasants who ploughed the land and ate what they raised were evicted from their lands and driven away from their villages, which became depopulated, while the lords turned the land into pasture for sheep, supporting a much smaller population, but yielding a much greater profit. Successive kings tried unsuccessfully to halt this process. On the other hand, the dissolution of the monasteries by Henry VIII aggravated it, since lands which had been responsibly farmed were bought up by speculators and were depopulated for wool production. This process meant that tens of thousands of previously more or less independent yeomen were deprived of a livelihood, a place to live, and the security of the village community on which they would otherwise have relied in time of need. They had no alternative but to head for the towns, seek work as wage labourers or, failing to find it, to become vagabonds and beggars.

Perhaps the most shameful feature of this whole history of expropriation is the way the state authorities treated these vagabonds. By Henry VIII's statute of 1530,

> They are to be tied to the cart-tail and whipped until the blood streams from their bodies, then to swear an oath to go back to their birthplace or to where they have lived the last three years, and to 'put themselves to labour'. (p. 734)

For the third offence, they were to be executed. The option of going back to their birthplace was of course not on, since their villages had often been razed to the ground, and not enough work was available in the towns. The stupid cast of mind behind this legislation we can still recognize well enough today in those who advocate harsher treatment of the unemployed as a remedy for unemployment, and write leaders in self-styled 'quality' papers to this effect. But the brutality of the punishments beggars belief. Elizabeth I and James I passed similarly brutal laws.

The process of expropriating the peasants did not stop with the Tudors. It was resumed on a massive scale in Scotland in the eighteenth-century 'highland clearances'. Heads of clans, who were traditionally the nominal holders of clan land, started treating the land as their private property, and evicting its population to make way for deer forests. ('Forest' here has its older sense of a place where deer may be hunted – no tree-planting took place.) This they did with the support of the Whig oligarchy and the English army. This was still going on in the early nineteenth century: Marx tells of the Duchess of Sutherland, who appropriated 794,000 acres of clan land, and between 1814 and 1820 evicted 15,000 inhabitants, having their houses burnt down. One old woman who refused to leave was burnt to death in her house.

The process resumed in England too in the eighteenth century, with the enclosure of land, whereby the rural population lost the commons where they had traditionally been able to collect wood and graze animals.

Marx goes on to discuss briefly the origin of the capitalist farmer, developing from the feudal bailiff to the large tenant farmer, and profiting too from the enclosures of the eighteenth century. He points out how the dispossession of the peasants facilitated capitalism not only by creating a propertiless proletariat, but by depriving the rural population of the ability to grow their own food, thus creating a home market. And he traces the origin of the industrial capitalist, not so much in the successful craftsman as in the merchant or banker who set up industry outside the guild-regulated towns.

Further primitive accumulation came about through the slave trade and the exploitation of Asian countries. 'In fact, the veiled slavery of the wage-workers in Europe needed, for its pedestal, slavery pure and simple in the new world' (pp. 759–60).

In the chapter called 'Historical tendency of capitalist accumulation', Marx fleshes out historically the point he makes in the passage I quote at the outset of the book. In the immediate pre-capitalist phase, there were many peasants and craftsmen who owned their own means of labour and thus were free in the work process, though they may have been exploited by landlords, merchants and usurers. Capitalism expropriates some by force and drives others out of business by competition, concentrating the means of production more and more into fewer and fewer hands. This process has advantages – co-operative labour, the application of science to production – but at the expense of the mass of people, who lose their freedom. Marx looks forward to this mass of people eventually 'expropriating the expropriators':

> The capitalist mode of appropriation, the result of the capitalist mode of production, produces capitalist private property. This is the first negation of individual private property, as founded on the labour of the proprietor. But capitalist production begets, with the inexorability of a law of Nature, its own negation. It is the negation of negation. This does not re-establish private property for the producer, but gives him individual property based on the acquisitions of the capitalist era: i.e. on co-operation and the possession in common of the land and of means of production.
>
> The transformation of scattered private property, arising from individual labour, into capitalist private property is, naturally, a process, incomparably more protracted, violent, and difficult, than the transformation of capitalistic private property, already practically resting on socialised production, into socialised property. In the former case, we had the expropriation of the mass of the people by a few usurpers; in the latter, we have the expropriation of a few usurpers by the mass of the people. (pp. 763–4)

Finally, Marx comes to another test case between his thinking and that of capitalist ideologists: the case of the 'colonies', in the traditional sense of that word, namely Australia and New Zealand. Capitalists took capital and workers to the colonies, only to discover that, since land was freely available, the workers rapidly transformed themselves into independent farmers and artisans, and the capital was no use since it could not buy labour-power. Apologists of capitalism see capital as the rightful property of the capitalist, ownership of which in no way encroaches on the rights of anyone else. But capital is useless if there are no propertiless proletarians whose labour-power it can buy. A certain Mr Peel, who took with him to Australia £50,000 of capital and 3000 proletarians found when he arrived that he 'was left without a servant to make his bed or fetch him water from the river' (p. 766). As Marx comments, 'He discovered that capital is not a thing, but a social relation between persons, established by the instrumentality of things.' In the mythology of capitalism, it differs from slavery and serfdom in that the capitalist's domination is not over people, but only over property. But it is a form of property that is only useful if it buys domination over people.

What made capitalist relations impossible in Mr Peel's situation? Simply the individual property of the workers. So individual property and capital, which are seen in capitalist propaganda as the same thing, are mutually incompatible. Consequently, those who wanted to re-establish capitalist relations of production in the colonies came up with the idea that the price of land there should be artificially raised above its market price, to keep the workers exploitable, which lets the cat out of the bag about the supposed 'naturalness' of capitalism.

What does this part of *Capital*, the final and perhaps the most easily readable part, actually prove? It certainly alters one's perception of English history: Henry VIII was not just beastly to his wives and counsellors, but to the poor among his people too; Elizabeth I didn't just kill Catholics and Baptists, but the chronically unemployed too. It also certainly proves that capitalism is not a 'natural' system, but depends historically upon the violent seizure of the means of life from the greater part of the people. But does it prove that capitalism today is unjust?

After all, we know that Bristol and Liverpool were built on the proceeds of the slave trade, but we do not conclude that those two great cities should be bulldozed down. The evil of the slave trade (*that* slave trade) is dead, and we rejoice both in its death and in any good that it might have left behind it.

One might accuse Marx of the 'genetic fallacy', that is, the idea that facts about the origin of something determine the value of it. But I think this would be mistaken. Marx is not saying that capitalism is bad because its origin is bad. That it *is* bad – whatever its origin – he has documented elsewhere, for instance in the chapter on the working day. But what he has done in this part of *Capital* is demolish an argument *for* capitalism which itself rests on the genetic fallacy, namely that which both the economists of his time and the recent philosophy of Robert Nozick offer: that capitalism is the consequence of a series of just transactions, and is therefore itself just.

The State, Democracy and Revolution

Marx's political thought in the narrow sense – his theory of the state – is dominated by two contrasts, which are linked together in various ways: the contrast between the different classes that may control the state; and the contrast between the state as an autonomous apparatus, and democracy. The latter has been seen by some Marxists as an inheritance from Rousseau, and to an extent it is. I shall look at the former first, as it is most characteristically Marxist.

In *The Communist Manifesto*, Marx says two things about the state which are sometimes mistakenly thought to be the same: (1) 'Political power, properly so called, is merely the organised power of one class for oppressing another' (*The Revolutions of 1848*, p. 87), and (2) 'The executive of the modern state is but a committee for managing the common affairs of the whole bourgeoisie' (p. 69).

The former is a general statement about all forms of state: in feudal monarchies the aristocratic classes oppress the peasants; in bourgeois democracies, or bourgeois dictatorships, the capitalists oppress the workers; in a workers' democracy, the workers oppress (that is, primarily, expropriate) the capitalists.

The latter quote quite explicitly refers to the 'modern representative state', for example the state as it existed in Britain after the Reform Bill – a state in which parliament had the real power, and was elected by the bourgeoisie.

Marx did not think that all states were merely executive committees of the ruling class. The absolute monarchies of the early modern period, for instance, represented a stage at which the bourgeoisie had, to a considerable extent, replaced the feudal classes, but was not yet strong enough to rule by itself. Landowners and bourgeois alike were protected in exploiting peasants and workers by these states. Likewise the military and bureaucratic states of Napoleon III and Bismarck were to be regarded by Marx as bourgeois states in which the bourgeoisie did not rule on its own account as in representative states, but nevertheless used the state to oppress the workers.

It should not be imagined, though, that these states which were not mere executive committees of the bourgeoisie were better than those that were; they were worse. This is because in them a double oppression takes place: of the working class by the ruling class, and of the whole of society by the state. In the 'executive committee' type of state on the contrary, the bourgeoisie still oppresses the proletariat, but the state is wholly subject to 'society', albeit bourgeois society. This brings us to the second issue, 'democracy versus the state apparatus', and to Marx's legacy from Rousseau. There is much in Rousseau that is muddled or mistaken, but one theory that is of great value: that although a state based on popular sovereignty must have a 'government', that is, a state apparatus, that government is in all cases a constant threat to popular sovereignty, as all governments tend to usurp sovereignty from the people if they get the chance. By 'sovereignty' Rousseau meant the right to legislate. This right should belong, according to Rousseau, not to representatives, but to the whole people. Rousseau's lasting contribution to political thought is his idea of measures to make this usurpation of sovereignty by government difficult. There are two sorts of such measures: (a) whatever can be done by the whole people should be – for example, a people's militia should replace standing armies; and (b) such specialized officials as are necessary should be elected. These are not legislators – the whole people is that – but they are administrators and enforcers.

Hence there is in Rousseau a sort of minimal state theory, different from the minimal state of liberalism. The liberal minimal state means minimal legislation. Rousseau's means minimal state apparatus. In this sense, Marx is a minimal statist too. It is noteworthy that in the text where he goes furthest in allowing the possibility of a peaceful road to socialism, the speech of the First International to the Hague Congress in 1872 (a year after the Paris Commune), he says:

> We know that heed must be paid to the institutions, customs and traditions of the various countries, and we do not deny that there are countries, such as America and England, and if I was familiar with its institutions, I might include Holland, where the workers may attain their goal by peaceful means. That being the case, we must recognize that in most continental countries the lever of revolution will have to be force. (*The First International and After*, p. 324)

So surprisingly enough in Britain, which did not have manhood suffrage and only a minority of workers could vote, a peaceful road is possible, whereas in Germany, which did have manhood suffrage, it is not. The difference is that in Britain while the 'people' in Rousseau's sense was still restricted to the property owners (household suffrage), that people was (albeit through its representatives), pretty much sovereign. In Germany, the monarchy, bureaucracy and army had a lot more power. So, once the suffrage was won in Britain and a workers' majority elected, there would be no serious obstacle to socialist measures, while a workers' majority in Germany would be at the mercy of the Kaiser's army. This becomes clearer if we look at the effect of the Paris Commune on Marx's thinking.

Until the Paris Commune of 1871, Marx, while making it clear that workers' power could only take the form of a democracy, did not say much about how that democracy would differ from bourgeois parliamentarism, except that the workers' party would be in the majority. But in his address on the Paris Commune, *The Civil War in France*, he holds up the Commune as an example of workers' democracy.

> The Commune was formed of municipal councillors, chosen by universal suffrage in the various wards of the town, responsible and revocable at short terms. The majority of its members were naturally working men, or acknowledged representatives of the working class. The Commune was to be a working, not a parliamentary body, executive and legislative at the same time. (*The First International and After*, p. 209)

It may not be strictly true that the workers had a majority: the two working-class groups, the Internationalists and the Blanquists, even together, were in a minority. But the artisan and shopkeeping petty bourgeoisie, who elected the rest of the Commune, were close to the proletariat in interests, as well as lifestyle. The bourgeoisie proper had either fled the city, or elected representatives who did not take their seats, and were later replaced in by-elections. But in calling the Commune 'a working, not a parliamentary body' Marx is indicating that it took on, not just the legislative functions of a parliament, but the functions of the heads of administration as well. And the Rousseauite measures noted above were implemented: 'Like the rest of public servants, magistrates and judges were to be elective, responsible, and revocable' (*The First International and After*, p. 210). 'The Commune made that catchword of bourgeois revolutions, cheap government, a reality, by destroying the two greatest sources of expenditure – the standing army and state functionarism' (p. 212).

When Marx says that 'the working class cannot simply lay hold of the ready-made state machinery, and wield it for its own purposes' (p. 206) he means that the hierarchic state apparatus with its top-down appointments must be replaced by representative democracy. In the first draft of the book, he calls the Commune 'the reabsorption of the state power by society as its own living forces instead of as forces controlling and subduing it' (p. 250), and says, 'It was a revolution against the *state* itself, this supernaturalist abortion of society, a resumption by the people for the people of its own social life' (p. 249), and in the final version refers to 'the new Commune, which breaks the modern state power' (p. 211).

Thus Marx links in his account of the Commune the contrast 'state over society–society over state' with the contrast 'bourgeois state–workers' state'. We have seen that he thought that even a bourgeois state could be of a non-parasitic 'society over state' sort, and it was precisely when this was the case that a socialist revolution could occur peacefully in it. It is noteworthy here that Marx objects to the phrase 'the free state' in his *Critique of the Gotha Programme*. The objection is somewhat pedantic, as no doubt what the German social democrats meant by a free state was a republic, but they could not say that legally. But Marx's point is clearly expressed by Engels in a letter to the German social democratic leader Bebel on the same issue:

> Taken in its grammatical sense, a free state is one where the state is free in relation to its citizens, hence a state with a despotic government. The whole talk about the state should be dropped, especially since the Commune, which was no longer a state in the proper sense of the word. (*Selected Works in One Volume*, p. 339)

But this workers' state is clearly seen as being even more 'society over state' – even less of a 'free state' than the best bourgeois state. Lenin is not wrong to say,

> The Commune, therefore, appears to have replaced the smashed state machine 'only' by fuller democracy: abolition of the standing army; all officials to be elected and subject to recall. But as a matter of fact this 'only' signifies a gigantic replacement of certain institutions by other institutions of a fundamentally different type. This is exactly a case of 'quantity being transformed into quality': democracy, intro-duced as fully and consistently as is at all conceivable, is transformed from bourgeois to proletarian democracy; from the state (= a special force for the suppression of a particular class) into something which is no longer the state proper. (Lenin, *Selected Works*, p. 293)

The necessary condition of a workers' state then is that the old state is smashed in the sense of its specialized hierarchies being abolished and replaced by democratic institutions. But though this is 'no longer a state in the proper sense of the word', it is still a state in some sense of the word, since this process of smashing the (bourgeois) state is distinct from the process of the new, workers' state 'withering away', which Marx and Engels also expect will happen. To this we must now turn our attention.

The phrase 'the withering away of the state' comes from Engels (indeed, from the older translations of Engels – more recent ones speak of its 'dying out'), but the idea is there in both Marx and Engels from the start. Engels introduces the phrase in this way:

> The first act by virtue of which the state really constitutes itself the representative of the whole of society – the taking possession of production in the name of society – this is, at the same time, its last

independent act as a state. State interference in social relations becomes, in one domain after another, superfluous, and then withers away of itself; the government of persons is replaced by the administration of things, and by the conduct of processes of production. The state is not 'abolished'. *It withers away.* (*Anti-Dühring*, p. 333)

This view is adumbrated in *The Communist Manifesto*:

When, in the course of development, class distinctions have disappeared, and all production has been concentrated into the hands of a vast association of the whole nation, the public power will lose its political character ...

In place of the old bourgeois society, with its classes and class antagonisms, we shall have an association, in which the free development of each is the condition for the free development of all. (*The Revolutions of 1848*, p. 87)

It is made more explicit at the end of Marx's essay 'On the alleged splits in the International' (1872). Marx in a sense owns up to being an anarchist in his final aims:

To all socialists anarchy means this: the aim of the proletarian movement – that is to say the abolition of social classes – once achieved, the power of the state, which now serves only to keep the vast majority of producers under the yoke of a small minority of exploiters, will vanish, and the functions of government become purely administrative. (*The First International and After*, p. 314)

The withering away of the state clearly presupposes the abolition of classes, for while they exist, the proletariat needs the state – albeit one that is not a state 'in the proper sense of the word', to prevent counter-revolution.

The question, What differentiates Marx from the anarchists? is a complex one. The obvious difference is that for Marx there has to be a transition period in between capitalism and anarchy, in which the workers are the ruling class. This 'two stages' theory is also linked to what Marx says about the distribution of goods. In his critique of the notion of 'equal right' in the *Critique of the Gotha Programme*, he suggests that in the early stages of socialism the main criterion determining one's share in the social consumption is the work one has done. But,

In a more advanced phase of communist society, when the enslaving subjugation of individuals to the division of labour, and thereby the antitheses between intellectual and physical labour, have disappeared; when labour is no longer just a means of keeping alive but has itself become a vital need; when the all-round development of individuals has also increased their productive powers and all the springs of co-operative wealth flow more abundantly – only then can society wholly cross the narrow horizon of bourgeois right and inscribe on its banner: From each according to his abilities, to each according to his needs! (*The First International and After*, p. 347)

William Morris and Lenin both (independently, I think) reserved the word 'communism' for this advanced stage, and called the less advanced one 'socialism', though this usage has no basis in Marx. The assumption of all three is that, under 'communism' in this sense, the state will have withered away.

This two-stage theory raises three questions.

1. If Marx (as we may assume) agrees with Engels that the public power in the first stage – the Commune-state – is already not a state in the proper sense of the word, what is it that has been abolished at this stage, and what has not?
2. In the second stage, what else has withered away, and what has not?
3. What is the relation between the two stages?

The account of the Paris Commune goes some way towards answering the first question: the standing army has been abolished and replaced by a citizens' militia, other parts of the state apparatus – judges, police chiefs, administrators – have become to a much larger extent elective posts. Democracy has been extended at the expense of the hierarchic state apparatus.

As to what is present in stage one but absent from stage two, the main part of the answer seems to be *coercion*. The workers' state has to force the capitalists to yield up their property, and suppress any 'pro-slavery rebellion', as Engels calls the predicted counter-revolutionary attempts, on analogy with the American Civil War. When there are no classes this sort of coercion becomes redundant. (Whether individual crime would die out, and if not how it would be dealt with, is an issue that Lenin and William Morris speculate about briefly in their very different ways, but Marx hardly mentions the problem; he does say, in an article in the *New York Tribune* against capital punishment, that none of the philosophical justifications for punishment work, and perhaps implies that society is to blame for crime, and that it would die out in a good society [Feuer, ed. *Marx and Engels: Basic Writings on Politics and Philosophy*, pp. 523–6].)

But what does not wither away is representative democracy; democracy as a form of state – that is, of coercion – does, but it is assumed that voting and elections will continue. Engels argues that the captain of a ship might be elected, but there still has to be a captain. Some anarchists, I think, would accept this idea, others not.

On the question of the relation between the two stages, we have different interpretations of Marx in William Morris and in Lenin and, oddly enough, Lenin's is more conducive to democratic liberties. For Morris they are related as means and end: what we aim for is the stateless communist society, which is depicted with great charm in *News from Nowhere*; we endure the transitional Commune-state as a necessary means, as we endure a surgical operation as a means to restored health. The problem with this is that means tend to become ends in themselves, and we may be sceptical about whether the second stage will ever come. Lenin, on the other hand, in his writings of 1917, makes it clear that the transitional state can begin to wither away from day one, since it only has to suppress a small minority, and must be so constituted that it inevitably withers away as long as it exists. This is in sharp contrast to Stalin's view that the state would go on becoming more powerful for some time before it withered away. I am inclined to attribute Lenin's interpretation to Marx himself, on the grounds that his critique of utopianism means that we should look at any transitional state, not in terms of its end, but in terms of its current developmental tendency. Regretfully, it has to be said that Lenin was unable to deliver a state that was inherently withering away, mainly because of causes outside his control.

But aside from the contingencies of the Russian or any other revolution, is the idea of the state withering away at all plausible? I have already suggested that this withering away should be seen as a process inherent in any genuinely socialist state rather than as an end product to be brought about. It seems to me quite plausible that there should be a state in which more and more public functions were performed by autonomous associations rather than central government, in which less and less coercion was necessary, in which the state apparatus was getting smaller and smaller. I doubt that this could lead to an end product in which there was no state at all; but it might approach it asymptotically.

There is one more thing that needs to be said about Marx's conception of democracy. Where there is a large and complex organization, such as a nation state, there can be two views about the most democratic way to organize it. According to one view, you establish full democracy at the top – an elected parliament or president – and ensure strict subordination at all lower echelons. This will mean, however, that the internal structure of the state's organizations will be hierarchic rather than democratic. Alternatively, you can democratize throughout, even though this will mean that partial organizations (local or functional) will have some autonomy from the democratic 'sovereign'. Consider the question of what democracy would mean in a university. Does it mean self-government through discussion and voting – what used to be called 'collegiality'? Or does it mean subordination to managers who are subordinate to civil servants who are subordinate to a minister who is subordinate to the prime minister who is (supposedly) subordinate to an elected parliament? The impression one gets from The Communist Manifesto is that Marx favours the centralized form, as he urges centralization of the state (perhaps in opposition to the division of Germany into backward petty autocracies). But, even at that time, he favoured a militia, not a standing army, and in the texts written after the Commune, the idea of democracy pervading administration rather than merely heading it seems to emerge. The question becomes sharper if one asks it in the context of economic democracy (alias socialism). Does it mean, as the quote at the beginning of this book seems to indicate, workers' control, industrial democracy? Or does it mean a command economy under a democratic parliament? It should be noted that even in Marx's most centralizing texts, it is political, not economic centralization that he is advocating, and in his response to the Commune, this too has gone. He does speak of state ownership in the programme of reforms at the end of *The Communist Manifesto*, but he is referring to the 'commanding heights', to banks and railways, not the whole of production. Writing about labour under socialism, he calls it 'freely associated labour', which suggests associationist socialism rather than state socialism. In the *Critique of the Gotha Programme*, he opposes state control of education, though he accepts state financing and inspection of it. In his notes on Bakunin he writes, 'With collective ownership the so-called people's will vanishes, to make way for the real will of the co-operative', which suggests that democracy is to be inherent in real, ongoing functional organizations, rather than in general elections every five years – a 'democracy all through' model, not a 'democracy at the top' model. The identification of socialism with state control is often blamed on Marx, but there have been many socialists, some of whom have been Marxists, who have held that autonomous democratic industrial associations should run industry. The exigencies of the Russian Civil War led Communists to state socialism – though even then the Workers' Opposition of Alexandra Kollontai and others called for turning industry over to the trade unions. And until the 'Morrison model' of monolithic state corporations was adopted by the postwar Labour government, there was a lively tradition of guild socialism – belief in the management of socialized industries by chartered associations of workers – on the English left. Marx is arguably more amenable to such associationist socialism, since it is certainly more likely that the state will be withering away if its managerial functions in industry are much reduced than if it has a huge concentration of economic power. I am far from thinking that state socialism is a total failure – by and large it has done better than private capital, as the British railways illustrate in their homely way, and a comparison of Cuban and American literacy rates in a more striking way. But if Marx is to be given his due in the twenty-first century, it is as the philosopher of economic democracy, not as the philosopher of state control.

Now we come to the question of how Marx's theory of the state and democracy affects his view of revolution, its necessity or otherwise. We have already seen that the need for revolution comes from the existence of powerful hierarchical state apparatuses – especially standing armies – even in states with parliaments elected by universal suffrage. The election of a socialist majority in such a state would lead, not to a peaceful transition to socialism, but to a bloody transition to an anti-socialist military dictatorship, as happened in Chile.

On the other hand, in a bourgeois parliamentary state without a standing army or a powerful bureaucracy, such a transition would be possible, as Marx says of Britain, USA and Holland. But we may ask – as Lenin asked in 1917 – whether there are any such states today. Lenin concludes that: 'Both Britain and America, the biggest and last representatives – in the whole world – of Anglo-Saxon "liberty", in the sense that they had no militarist cliques and bureaucracy' (Lenin, Selected Works, p. 290) have acquired both and lost that liberty. No one listening to what some leading British Conservatives have said about Pinochet's coup can doubt that they would be in the forefront of a similar coup if a socialist (as distinct from a Labour) government were elected in Britain.

Appendix: Marx's blind spot about nationalism

I intend the metaphor of a blind spot to be taken seriously; Marx's social vision was very clear over most of the visual field; he remains in my view the greatest political thinker of all time; even today, reading Capital is the first necessity if you want to understand the world; but he had one or two blind spots, of which the most far-reaching within political theory was his massive underestimation of the power of nationalism.

This affects his social theory, not just his personal attitudes. When he analysed the capitalist economy he was quite clear about the fact that to understand the behaviour of a capitalist firm you had to recognize two struggles in which it was necessarily engaged: with its workers, to keep their hours long and their wages low; and with other capitalist firms, for a larger share of the market. But when he analyses the state, he considers only its relations with its own people. Yet he should have known as a Hegel scholar, or indeed from observation of current events, that a state is also defined by its relations with other states, and huge portions of the state apparatus exist because of these relations of diplomacy, war, trade, and so on.

I am sure that the explanation for missing this crucial feature of states is that he thought nation states were already on their way out:

> National one-sidedness and narrow-mindedness become more and more impossible, and from the numerous national and local literatures there arises a world literature. (p. 209)
>
> The workingmen have no country. (ibid)
>
> National differences and antagonisms between peoples are daily more and more vanishing, owing to the development of the bourgeoisie, to freedom of commerce, to the world market, to uniformity in the mode of production and in the conditions of life corresponding thereto. (p. 225)
>
> [Communists] labour for the union and agreement of the democratic parties of all countries. (ibid)
>
> Workingmen of all countries, unite! (p. 241)
>
> (All quotes from 'The Communist Manifesto', in *Selected Works in Two Volumes*, vol. 1, Lawrence and Wishart, 1942)

Marx clearly favours internationalism and wants the workers' movement to be international: about this I have no criticism. But he also thinks that the bourgeoisie is already – in 1847 – transcending nationalism and building a united world. Nationalism is seen as a dying enemy which need not be taken seriously. And this seems to be Marx's personal attitude. He was an exemplary internationalist, speaking many languages and writing in three of them, and being German by birth, French by citizenship and English by residence. Yet he was not a tetchily 'politically correct' internationalist. He and his family would sing German patriotic songs on their way home from their Sunday afternoon picnics on Hampstead Heath. He just didn't regard nationalism as a strong enough enemy to be taken seriously.

He could not have been more wrong. The heyday of nationalism was still to come: the unification of Germany and Italy, the 1914–18 war, the independence of the Eastern European states, the rise of Fascism, the 1939–45 war, the spread of nationalism to the previously colonized countries. Even today, when national sovereignty in Europe is beginning to be eroded by federalism, nationalist ideology is very powerful. Consider the fact that those British Muslims who opted to fight for Taliban in Afghanistan have (at the time I write this) recently been described as 'traitors'. They no doubt sincerely believed that they were obliged to do what they did by loyalty to Islam. No religious believer could put national loyalty above loyalty to their religion. But the use of the epithet 'traitor' suggests that it is thought that they should. This indicates that nationalism is the religion of those who use the word 'traitor' in this context, even if they hypocritically take communion in a Christian church.

Why was Marx so blind to the virulent power of nationalism? I don't think it is fully explained by his own internationalism, of which more in a minute. I think that it is partly due to the fact that, despite his internationalism, he was affiliated to a political and philosophical tradition which was itself nationalist, namely the tradition that starts with Enlightenment political philosophers like Hobbes, Spinoza, Locke and Rousseau and finds its climax in the French Revolution. In economic terms this movement is capitalist as against feudal and in political terms individualist as against organicist; in ideological terms, it is nationalist; as against what? I think the answer can only be: as against Christian. Its point is the same as that of those who call the British Taliban fighters traitors: that one's first loyalty should be to one's nation-state not one's religion. To its philosophical defenders this looks innocent enough: it is supposedly justified by the still real problem of religious persecution and the myth of the religious wars of the sixteenth and seventeenth centuries. I call it a myth because these wars were much more dynastic and nationalist than religious: His Catholic Majesty of France fought on the Protestant side in the Thirty Years' War. The assumption of Spinoza and Rousseau is that, if everyone gives their first allegiance to the state, all the religions within the state can tolerate one another. But this misses the point that no religious believer can give his or her first allegiance to the state. So, instead of a prescription for universal tolerance, it is a prescription for persecution of all religions. On this rock the French Revolution crashed: a revolution that had the consensus of the Third Estate behind it became a revolution resisted by the Catholic half of the people, and consequently a revolution that had to live by terror. Marx was raised in a culture formed by this revolution, which had extended to the Rhineland where he was born. He inherited its secularism, but not the nationalism which was the positive side of that secularism, since to inherit that he would have to have been a French nationalist, and he was a German. In the Enlightenment and the French Revolution, secularism and nationalism were a unitary phenomenon, negative and positive sides of the same thing. In inheriting the negative side of this only, Marx cannot see the positive side because he is at once too outside it to share it and too inside it to observe it. Hence he stitches together a mismatched garment in his conception of bourgeois society: capitalist in economics, individualist in political thought, religious in ideology. He does not see that in bourgeois society at least, not religion but nationalism is the opium of the people, the dominant ideology that enables the bourgeoisie to keep the workers loyal. (Today, perhaps even this is becoming outdated: consumerism is the new opium of the people.)

(For an alternative – and much fuller – account of Marx on nationalism, see Erica Benner's *Really Existing Nationalisms*.)

Marx and Philosophy

Marx was, by training, a philosopher. He studied philosophy at university, and obtained a doctorate for a thesis on ancient Greek philosophy. He writes like a philosopher: the attention to the analysis of concepts and their precise use, the logical structure of his arguments, all show the methods and skills of a philosopher to a high degree. His reputation today is probably higher among philosophers than in any other academic discipline, and deservedly so: in his manner of argument, he is a philosopher, and one of the greatest. Yet from 1845 on, the subject matter of his writing is not, for the most part, philosophy, but social science and political commentary. Much of what he says in 1845 gives the impression of consciously turning his back on philosophy. For instance (to take the most extreme example):

> One has to 'leave philosophy aside' ... one has to leap out of it and devote oneself like an ordinary man to the study of actuality ... Philosophy and the study of the actual world have the same relation to one another as onanism [masturbation] and sexual love. ('The German Ideology', *Collected Works*, vol. 5, p. 236)

There have always been some Marxists – and, at times, Engels comes close to being one of them – who have proclaimed that with Marx, philosophy comes to an end, and is replaced by something else. I have been told by a philosopher who had studied in Eastern Europe under communism that the main emphasis there was on the history of philosophy. Philosophy was seen as having a very instructive history, but as no longer being a live discipline today. This is akin to the ideas of the positivist movement, which saw philosophy as the middle stage in the three-stage development of human thought, more advanced than religion, but now superseded by science. The last quote from Marx in 1845 comes close to positivism, yet Marx always had a higher opinion of philosophers such as Aristotle and Hegel than he did of the positivists.

To understand Marx's attitude to philosophy, one needs to understand two features of the philosophy in which Marx was trained – not just Hegel, but the whole tradition of European rationalism and idealism. The first is that it seeks to liberate humankind by basing everything on reason. It is in this sense that Descartes – though himself politically conservative by temperament – is often seen as the forerunner of the French Revolution. Kant defined the Enlightenment by the slogan *sapere aude!*, 'dare to use your own reason'. He sees political progress as an effect of this free rational discussion. To Hegel, the theme of human emancipation is quite explicit, even though deflected into the unlikely channel of support for the Prussian monarchy.

The second feature is that all of these philosophers thought that pure reason could tell you quite a lot about the world. In that sense, it was speculative: it relied on thinking rather than experience or experiment. In its earlier form – Descartes and Spinoza – it saw geometry, with its axioms and definitions, as the typical form of knowledge, on which others could be modelled. There is an apocryphal story that, when Hegel was lecturing on the philosophy of history, a history student in the class interrupted to say, 'But Herr Professor, the facts are different', to which Hegel, unruffled, replied, 'So much the worse for the facts.'

Marx's attitudes to each of these two aspects of philosophy as he knew it are very different. When in his early works he first talks about an end for philosophy, he is mainly thinking of the project of emancipation by reason, and he does not mean that philosophy should be superseded by science and laid aside; he means that what philosophy has projected theoretically – human emancipation based on reason – should be realized in practice. Philosophy, like the law in the teaching of Jesus, is not to pass away, but to be fulfilled. The fulfilment, however, will not itself be philosophy, but politics. At this stage, he says, 'You cannot transcend philosophy without realising it' (*Early Writings*, p. 250) and, 'Just as philosophy finds its *material* weapons in the proletariat, so the proletariat finds its *intellectual* weapons in philosophy' (*Early Writings*, p. 257).

When he talks about philosophy in *The German Ideology*, however, he is thinking of philosophy as speculation, and saying that this is no way to find out how the world works. If the facts contradict the theory, so much the worse, not for the facts, but for the theory. We have seen in connection with the eleventh thesis on Feuerbach that he is urging us to turn, not from an old philosophy to a new philosophy, nor from theory to practice, but from speculative philosophy to empirical social science.

Marx's turn from speculation to social scientific enquiry did not, in fact, mean that his later works had no philosophical content. The history of social science has proved again and again that the alternative to having a suitable philosophy of social science is not having no philosophy but having a bad philosophy. From this, Marx's philosophical education saved him. For, once he gets down to really substantial work in the social sciences, he inevitably encounters philosophical problems, and he is ready for them. This shows most clearly in the methodological introductions that he wrote from time to time.

For when, in his mature work, Marx 'gets philosophical', the reason is generally some problem of methodology in the social sciences that he has encountered in his explanatory work in that area. Let us start with one, very short, two-sentence example of this. In the Preface to the First German edition of *Capital*, Marx writes, 'In the analysis of economic forms ... neither microscopes nor chemical reagents are of use. The force of abstraction must replace both' (*Capital*, vol. 1, Moore/Aveling translation, p. 8). In other words, experiments, in the sense that the experimental sciences use them, are not available to social science. But the work that experiments do for sciences where they are available, needs to be done in those sciences where they are not. What does an experiment do? It cordons off the natural mechanism to be tested from irrelevant variables. For instance, if you were testing the boiling point of water, you would need to ensure that the water was pure, since salt or alcohol in it would alter the boiling point, and that you were at sea level, since height above sea level alters the air pressure and therefore the boiling point of water. This is possible, since we can eliminate impurities in water, and take it to a place at sea level. But in economics (or any other human science) we cannot eliminate the 'impurities' – for instance the effects of politics or of weather on the economy. We can choose the most favourable conditions for testing a theory – hence, as we have seen, Marx's focus on industries with no legal limits to exploitation. But this only partly eliminates the irrelevant variables. The rest must be done by 'the power of abstraction', that is, by bracketing off irrelevant variables *in thought*, recognizing that when we come to apply the thought to reality, these variables will be back in place affecting the outcome.

What sort of thing must the social world be for such bracketing off to be necessary and possible? Marx throws some light on this in his 1857 Introduction. In the section called 'The Method of Political Economy', he tells us that

> The concrete is concrete because it is the concentration of many determinations, hence unity of the diverse. It may appear in the process of thinking, therefore, as a process of concentration, as a result, not as a point of departure, even though it is the point of departure in reality, and hence also the point of departure for observation and conception. (*Grundrisse*, p. 101)

In other words, concrete realities – say a society – are complex wholes, in which many processes interact to produce the outcome. To understand such a concrete reality, one must understand all the different processes and their interaction. So thinking about (say) a society must start from these many processes. They, however, are not immediately visible to us. We start by observing a concrete society, and analysing it to discover the many processes. When we have formed concepts of these, we start the process of thought that shows how they are connected to form the complex whole of society. At the end we have a complex idea of society, which hopefully maps the real society; but to get there, we have to pass through the stage of analysis, abstracting the particular processes from their places in the whole – though of course they could not really occur apart from the whole; this abstraction or separation occurs only in thought.

Three philosophical features of this method can be noted: it is realist, that is, it aims to map in thought things that exist outside thought, in the real world; it is oriented towards wholes, not atoms (of which more shortly); and it regards these wholes as analysable complexes, not simple wholes that cannot be analysed without falsification.

These methodological passages can be seen as expressing a wider philosophical outlook. Although the mature Marx wrote little specifically about philosophy, it is often claimed that there is a philosophy implicit in his work, and there have been various attempts at spelling out this philosophy. The earliest and most well-known of these attempts occurs in the work of Engels, Plekhanov and Lenin, and is usually called 'dialectical materialism'. This is not a bad description of Marx's philosophical approach, although he himself never used this phrase. It was in fact invented by Joseph Dietzgen, a German worker-philosopher who drew on some of the same sources as Marx, and was well-regarded by Marx and, more particularly, Engels. The phrase came into general currency during the time of the Second International (1889–1914), largely as a result of the work of Plekhanov, the founder of Russian Marxism and, in my view, a powerful and much under-rated thinker. After the Russian Revolution (which, incidentally, Plekhanov opposed as premature), dialectical materialism (contracted to the Newspeak word 'diamat'), became the official philosophy of the Soviet Union and the Third International; this naturally had a stifling effect on it as a tradition of critical thinking. Some rather vague, and useful enough, rules of thumb, which Engels had formulated as 'laws of dialectic', came to be treated as dogmas that could be applied to everything. Though it can be said that, despite its schematic and uncritical nature, this 'diamat' did avoid most of the most serious mistakes that other twentieth century philosophies fell into.

I shall say no more here about the later development of dialectical materialism. However, the two component parts of the phrase, 'dialectic' and 'materialism' do sum up the main components of Marx's philosophical approach. I will devote the next part of this chapter to discussing them in turn.

Dialectic

In origin, the word 'dialectic' is related to 'dialogue'. In the Middle Ages, philosophy was often called dialectic, which is a good word for it since, if one wanted to define the subject matter of philosophy, the best shot at it might be 'whatever issues can be resolved, if at all, by dialogue rather than by experiment or calculation'.

This root meaning of dialectic lies behind the special sense given it by Hegel, and partly taken over by Marx. Suppose a group of people, all with different experiences of the world, are engaged in a dialogue to seriously attempt to find the truth about something. Typically, one will put forward one view, which will have some truth in it, but be one-sided. Another will contradict by putting forward an alternative idea, which will also be part of the truth, but one-sided in a different way. If all goes well, they will between them arrive at a fuller view, which incorporates the element of truth in both their views. This will still be only a partial truth however, but fuller than the two views it replaces. It will form the starting point of a new dialogue, in which a contrary view will be counterposed to it, and a fuller view still arrived at by dialogue between the two. Thus knowledge progresses from partial, one-sided truths to fuller truths, without ever arriving at a final, complete truth. Many commentators label the stages of this process – an idea, its contradicting idea, and the fuller idea that contains the truth in both – as 'thesis, antithesis, synthesis' (although these terms are not particularly Hegelian or Marxian).

For Hegel, not only is there progress of knowledge among a group of individuals by dialogue; but the progress of human civilization, which (for him) is founded on progress of knowledge, happens in a similar way. The French Revolution, for instance, posits the idea of basing all human institutions on reason; that is the thesis. The reaction against it in England and Germany, which emphasizes the historical basis of all institutions in an organic development of communities, is the antithesis. Hegel's own social philosophy, perhaps, is the synthesis. However, none of these are just ideas, though the ideas for Hegel are crucial. The French Revolution is also a political and economic reality, as is the reaction against it. The synthesis is not just Hegel's philosophy, but the corporate constitutional state that Hegel always, though vainly, expected to be established by the Prussian monarchy, which paid him his professor's salary. And the dialogue was not just a conversation, but the Napoleonic War.

There is a similar pattern to Marx's account of the development of the capitalist economy and its supersession by socialism. The thesis might be individual craft production, where the workers are free because they own their own means of labour, but productivity is low. The antithesis is capitalism, which expropriates the craftworkers and replaces them with large-scale production, in which many co-operate, that has a high technology and therefore productivity, but leaves the workers unfree because they are compelled to sell their labour-power as they own no means of labour. The synthesis is socialism, retaining from capitalism the highly productive technology and the large-scale co-operation which is essential to it, but freeing the workers by making them the collective owners of their means of labour.

However, when Marx talks about dialectic he generally focuses on two concepts that we have already met in political contexts: contradiction and inversion. For instance, to use an example from *Capital* that is even more relevant today, capitalism as it advances demands both that the workers restrict themselves to more and more specialized skills in an extreme form of the division of labour, and also demands adaptability to new skills, since its technology constantly changes. Here are two demands, both necessary for the successful working of the same system, but mutually incompatible: an inner contradiction of capitalism. We have already seen examples of inversion from Marx's early writings: the product comes to dominate the producer. But, having acquainted ourselves with the section on 'primitive accumulation', we can see another kind of inversion: where an institution is transformed into its opposite. Private property in the means of labour – the condition of freedom for a peasant and craft community – becomes the means of enslavement of workers when the means of labour become too extensive to be owned by each worker, so that private property now means one person's property at the expense of the propertilessness of all the others. Hence,

> Capitalist production begets, with the inexorability of a law of Nature, its own negation. It is the negation of negation. This does not re-establish private property for the producer, but gives him individual property based on the acquisitions of the capitalist era: i.e. on co-operation and the possession in common of the land and the means of production. (*Capital*, vol. 1, 1959, p. 76)

This theory of contradictions and inversions is far from the general-ized theory of dialectic that is often attributed to Marx: it is a set of very specific claims about particular aspects of particular societies. However, in one way, it does have more far-reaching implications.

Let us take the contradiction most central to Marx's thought: class struggle in capitalist society. Unlike some conflicts – for instance, between Vikings and Saxons in the early Middle Ages – this is a conflict between two groups whose existence as the groups they are is dependent on their relation to the other group: there can be no bourgeoisie without a proletariat and no proletariat without a bour-geoisie. So we have here to do with conflict between interdependent, internally related classes. Now there are two – opposite – conceptions of the nature of society on which such conflict would make no sense. There is the atomistic view that society does not exist, only individ-uals exist. Hence the conflict of bourgeoisie and proletariat would be no different from that of Vikings and Saxons, who were not inter-defined parts of a common whole. On the other hand, there is the view that society as a whole is such a coherent unity that it cannot generate contradictory groups or tendencies. As against both of these views, Marx sees society as a composite reality, the whole defining the positions of its parts, but not wholly determining its parts. A prole-tarian is a proletarian because of his or her position in society, but if proletarians did not also have individual needs and capacities not assigned them by society, they would never find it necessary to rebel against capitalist society.

Marx is often seen as an extremist and, in political terms, he is obviously an extremist in one sense, that is, he is quite a long way left of centre. But in philosophical disputes, Marx is quite often in a position between two extremes, and this is a case in point. He does not agree with Benito Mussolini that the individual is nothing but an aspect of society; neither does he agree with Margaret Thatcher that there is no such thing as society, only individuals. Society is composed, rather, of the relations between individuals, but individuals' powers are restricted, and to some extent given, by their place in these relations. And this conception of society is an aspect of dialectic, in that the central dialectical concept of contradiction could have no place without it.

One does not find anywhere in Marx the idea of dialectic as a feature of everything, or as a single process with a predetermined outcome – both ideas which commentators often attribute to him. The idea of a universal dialectic, which is present in Hegel, is introduced into Marxism by Engels, and survives in later formalized 'diamat'. What Marx would have thought of it, we simply do not know.

Materialism

While the word 'dialectic' is rarely used today except in connection with Marxism, 'materialism' has a lot of uses which are nothing to do with Marx's materialism. First of all, in common colloquial English, materialism means valuing material possessions above other things. In this sense, Marx is certainly not a materialist. Indeed, he valued the mental capacities of humankind above anything else. Paul Lafargue relates that he was fond of quoting a saying of Hegel's: 'Even the criminal thought of a scoundrel is grander and more sublime than the wonders of the heavens' ('Reminiscences of Marx', in *Selected Works in Two Volumes*, vol. 1, p. 87). He would have regarded materialism in the popular sense as a feature of capitalist lifestyle.

Secondly, most materialist philosophers before Marx were what Marxists have always called mechanistic or metaphysical materialists. They believed that the ultimate reality is bits of matter colliding with one another and affecting each other according to mechanical laws. Marx was not a materialist of this kind; he did not think that the laws of the organic and social world could be reduced to the laws of mechanics. What is called materialism in philosophy departments today is a descendant of this mechanistic materialism, which Marx rejected.

Perhaps, as in the case of dialectic, it is best to start with the very concrete, applied uses of this concept, and then branch out to discuss its wider philosophical implications. Materialism for Marx means first and foremost the idea that *existence precedes consciousness*, that is, that our ideas about the world come from our interaction as living organisms with the world as our environment. The main way in which this idea is used by Marx is in arguing that we should explain the culture of a society in terms of the way it makes its living from nature rather than vice versa. The whole base-superstructure model is an outworking of this idea. This is the sense that the term 'materialism' has in the phrase 'the materialist conception of history' (or 'historical materialism' for short) – the term by which Marx and Engels referred to their theory of history. I think it is clear that materialism in this sense is absolutely fundamental to Marx's whole work.

But the slogan 'existence precedes consciousness' has other ramifications as well. Insofar as Marx has an argument for it, it is that the physical world existed before life, which depends on it, and life existed before consciousness, which depends on the interaction of living organisms with their natural environment. Hence Marx's 'ontology', that is, his theory of what there is, and of the causal ordering of different kinds of being, is a materialist one. Along with materialism in this sense goes Marx's atheism, for theism asserts that God's consciousness existed before matter or nature generally. However, it is quite possible to think that Marx was right about the ordering of matter, life and consciousness in nature, while holding that nature as a whole is created by God. Marx probably thought that atheism was a much more essential feature of his thought than it actually was. (Both he and Engels opposed attempts to *impose* atheism, whether upon members of the International or upon citizens of a future socialist state. The persecution of religion practised by some 'communist' governments has no roots in Marx.)

Finally, materialism contrasts with idealism, the philosophy that, in one form or another, dominated German thought in Marx's time, particularly in his youth. Kant and Hegel are the most important German idealists. For their idealism, existence does not precede consciousness, since all we can know about existence we know through consciousness, and we know it only in the form that consciousness presents it to us. Those who think that this idealist argument works would not necessarily deny that planet Earth existed before there was life on it, or that life existed for many millions of years before consciousness did. But they would claim that all we can know about, for example, dinosaurs or the primal soup, is structured by the nature of the human mind; we are, so to speak, trapped inside consciousness.

That Marx finds this idealism unconvincing is perhaps due to his emphasis on *practice* rather than purely contemplative knowledge, as the main way in which we encounter reality. In practice, we do not just form ideas about the world, we bang our heads against it, and are forced to move beyond the constructs of our own minds.

> The question whether objective truth can be attributed to human thinking is not a question of theory but is a *practical* question. Man must prove the truth, i.e. the reality and power, the this-sidedness of his thinking in practice. The dispute over the reality or non-reality of thinking that is isolated from practice is a purely *scholastic* question. (Second Thesis on Feuerbach, *Early Writings*, p. 422)

> All social life is essentially *practical*. All mysteries which lead theory to mysticism find their rational solution in human practice and in the comprehension of this practice. (Eighth Thesis on Feuerbach, p. 423)

I think that Marx is saying that if we engage practically with the world, we are forced to recognize its reality; if we only engage with it theoretically, the idealists' argument looks plausible. I also think Marx is quite right about this, and argue this in my book *In Defence of Objectivity*. However, Marx himself does not develop the argument at any length. He has other fish to fry.

He did think, though, that even purely philosophical idealism could have bad effects on politics. This is shown by his little parable at the beginning of *The German Ideology*:

> Once upon a time a valiant fellow had the idea that men were drowned in water only because they were possessed with the idea of gravity. If they were to knock this idea out of their heads, say by stating it to be a

superstition, a religious concept, they would be sublimely proof against any danger from water. His whole life long he fought against the illusion of gravity, of whose harmful results all statistics brought him new and manifold evidence. This honest fellow was the type of the new revolutionary philosophers in Germany. (*The German Ideology*, ed. C.J. Arthur, p. 37)

The practical moral of this is that we cannot change the world by changing our heads. We need to get our hands dirty. I do not think that the position parodied here is in any way a 'straw man'. It hits both philosophers like Rorty, and a hundred-and-one popular books that you will find in the 'Body, mind and spirit' section of any modern bookshop.

So much for dialectic and materialism according to Marx. A variety of interpretations have been placed on Marx's philosophical position since his death. 'Dialectical materialism' is one. Ever since it became an official state philosophy, it lost its capacity to be critical as a philosophy should be. On other issues, Soviet politicians have not felt bound by Marx's or Engels's words. Stalin knew and stated that he was going against their ideas when he forcibly collectivized agriculture, and defended himself with words that many others have used since: 'There is dogmatic Marxism and creative Marxism; I stand by the latter.' But 'diamat' became largely a matter of 'proving' points by quotations from classic Marxist texts. Even so, dialectical materialism avoided many mistakes of most other modern philosophy. It remained realist in the strong sense of believing that there is a reality that is independent of the human mind, and that the human mind can know; and at the same time, that knowledge is always growing but will never reach a final state of absolute truth. It held to both the idea that people make their own history and the idea that history is a law-governed process, and Plekhanov's account of how these two ideas are compatible is still worth reading.

But three other readings of Marx's philosophy should be mentioned. There is the sort that bases itself on the slogan 'the primacy of practice'. We have seen that, for Marx, this primacy meant that practical interaction with the world would keep our knowledge objective; however, it is often used to mean that our knowledge is trapped inside our practical concerns. It is used to justify stating practical principles first, and basing one's theoretical beliefs on them. We can see what Marx would have thought of this from his quarrel with Weitling. Weitling wanted to select economic theories on political grounds, rather than basing political practice on an analysis of capitalist society. Marx responded by banging the table and saying, 'Ignorance never helped anyone.'

Another version of Marxist philosophy reads Marx as remaining the left Hegelian that he was before 1845. This view also tends to go with playing down the claim to objective knowledge, and with seeing Marxism as essentially the expression of proletarian class consciousness rather than the uncovering of the nature of capitalist society. This view is exemplified by the early philosophy of the Hungarian Marxist Lukacs. Both these versions of Marxism leave it unclear why one should adopt Marxism in the first place; it seems like an arbitrary leap of faith rather than being convinced that Marx has the best account of the problems of capitalism and their solution.

The third interpretation goes to the other extreme. This is the view of the French Marxist philosopher Louis Althusser, who aims to return to Marx and derive a philosophy from what is implicit in *Capital* rather than either from Hegel or from Marx's explicitly philosophical remarks. In particular it rejects the early writings with their themes of humanism and alienation, and defends the scientific status of *Capital*. The philosophy that results is essentially a philosophy of science, and has been criticized for passing over issues of moral and political philosophy in silence. In my opinion, Althusser is preferable to the other two tendencies, but I feel that all three reconstructions contain more theoretical anomalies than Marx's original.

How, then, ought one to do philosophy after Marx? Marx's criticism of philosophies that try to tell you what the world is like in advance of any experience of it, is sound enough. We may well celebrate the end of *that sort* of philosophy. But then, English-speaking philosophy has usually rejected such views anyway – yet Marx showed little interest in English-speaking philosophy. Perhaps he thought that the main English-speaking tradition of philosophy – 'empiricism' – was right about its defining contention that we can know about the world only by experiencing it, and wrong about virtually everything else. Perhaps recent English-speaking philosophy – that of the second half of the twentieth century – has lost even that virtue: it has come to believe in 'conceptual truths', which are supposed to be true independently of experience, yet informative.

But it is possible to do philosophy without thinking that there is any special class of truths to which philosophy is the mode of access. Philosophy just means thinking hard about questions that matter but which cannot be resolved by experiment or calculation. Marx's work gives us some fine examples of philosophy so defined.

But why is this hard-thinking necessary? One reason is that our experience of the world, both in everyday life and in science, presents us with paradoxical conclusions – often with apparent contradictions: for instance, we think with our brains, yet thought appears to be autonomous and brain processes to be physically caused. Philosophy largely arises out of the attempt to resolve such contradictions. In the following chapter, I shall discuss three paradoxes in the thought of Marx himself, which have given rise to many philosophical discussions in both Marxist and anti-Marxist thought since.

Paradoxes in Marx's Thought?

There are various ways in which one might make a case against Marx. Some I shall mention but not discuss in any detail, as this would take me too far away from the subject of this book. But some are supposed paradoxes or contradictions within Marx's own thought, and these I will discuss at greater length in this chapter.

First, a brief list of objections other than the paradoxes, starting with the weakest. It is sometimes alleged – notably by Sir Karl Popper – that the whole basis of Marx's social science is unsound because it consists of prophecies, and sciences do not make prophecies. (Also it is alleged that the prophecies did not come true.) This, as we have seen, is based on a misreading of Marx, and so is a non-starter. While there are predictions of a kind in Marx, they are not 'prophecies' of what will happen whatever, but conditional predictions like those of other sciences: while certain structures remain in place, certain tendencies will continue to develop. More of this later in the chapter. Secondly, it is alleged that he just made the wrong hypotheses in social science – for instance it is denied that there is a ruling class in capitalist democracies, or that class struggle is the main motor of history. To assess these criticisms one would have to compare at length historical explanations made on the basis of Marx's theory and those of alternative theories, to see which explained the facts better. This is not the place to do that, though I may say in passing that I think Marx would win this contest. We have seen one example in the rival views of Marx and Weber about the relations between Protestantism and capitalism. Thirdly, it might be said that, however right Marx might be about capitalism, his socialist alternative is impracticable. Three main grounds are given for this: (1) That it is against human nature. We have already seen the weakness of this argument in chapters two and four. On the one hand, the next stage – socialism – does not require any contentious claims about human nature, but could work with people as they are. The more advanced stage – sometimes called communism – does depend on some contentious claims about human nature, but they are not implausible ones on the available evidence. (2) It is argued that large-scale planning must always be inefficient, as the knowledge needed for economic decision-making is scattered local knowledge and cannot be concentrated into a central planning agency. This argument, associated with the Austrian economist von Hayek, is a very serious one. In reply, it could be said that socialist decision-making is not necessarily more centralized than capitalist; capitalist firms can be bigger than nation states, and socialism could be decentralized to local communes and workers' councils, which would be able to tap local knowledge more effectively than a giant corporation. (3) It could be argued that the only way to establish socialism is by a civil war, and this would not only be a great evil in itself, but would inevitably end, not in a socialist democracy, but in a military or police dictatorship, worse than capitalist democracy. This is also a criticism that deserves respect, particularly in the light of twentieth-century history. It can be replied that some revolutions in the past have eventually led to democracy, and that the consequences of continued capitalism could be even worse – for example, the destruction of life on earth through environmental disasters.

Finally, we come to the alleged paradoxes internal to Marx's thought, which I shall discuss at some length. The first concerns Marx's claim to have founded a social science, combined with his tendency to explain away social theories as mere expressions of class interest or prejudice. The second is perhaps an instance of this, his apparent scepticism about morality combined with his denunciation of the immorality of capitalism. The third is his 'determinist' theory of history as a law-governed process, combined with his call to action, to change the world not merely interpret it.

Ideology and science

For Marx, ideology belongs to the 'superstructure', that is, it is in some way explained by the economic 'base' and the middling storeys such as politics. And all ideas presumably belong to this superstructural level, including scientific ideas. But this raises the problem: if ideas are explained, not by what they are about, but by their social base, are they worth anything? How can we know if they are true or not? For instance, Darwin's theory has sometimes been explained as a projection onto the natural world of capitalist competition in which 'the weakest go to the wall' or 'devil take the hindmost'. If Darwin's theory is explained by the society he lived in rather than by the facts about speciation, we have no reason to believe that it is true. Yet most people today – like Marx himself – do believe that Darwin's theory is true. And of course what applies to Darwin would apply to Marx himself: is his supposed social science merely the effect of some mechanism whereby the economic base determines what we think?

This problem becomes all the sharper because Marx does use the theory of ideology in this debunking way. The theories of (some) bourgeois economists are explained away as mere effects of the capitalist system, not insight into it. In part, this is an instance of a very common kind of debunking argument: 'they would say that, wouldn't they'. When, for example, scientists working for a chemical corporation report that its products are harmless, we do not believe them without independent confirmation. However, ideology, even when it does misrepresent the world, is not always conscious lying. 'The ruling ideas of each age have ever been the ideas of its ruling class' (*The Revolutions of 1848*, p. 85), but, though those ideas certainly serve the interests of the ruling class, they are also for the most part believed to be true by members of that class. Furthermore, not all ideological mystification comes from the ruling class. Marx's famous statement that religion is the opium of the people does not mean that it is a drug foisted on the oppressed by their oppressors; in context, it means that the oppressed take to religion to relieve their own sufferings, just as the Victorians – including Marx – used opium as a pain-killer or a tranquillizer. So ideas that Marx believes are false and likely to perpetuate oppression can arise from society in at least three ways: they can be purveyed as deliberate lies by the propagandists of the ruling class; they can be believed by the ruling class because their circumstances predispose them to believe them; or they can arise among the oppressed as a comfort.

Now several people have suggested that this debunking account of ideology in fact applies to Marx's own views too. Firstly, under the influence of Nietzsche, it has been argued that socialism and indeed democracy in general is an expression of the envy of the oppressed classes. Secondly, the anarchist Bakunin has claimed that Marx's version of socialism was the ideology of an intellectual élite in the working-class movement, which would form the nucleus of a new ruling class after the revolution, and that is one account of what has actually happened in the twentieth century. Both these views suggest that Marx or socialists generally are somehow to blame for what is a correctable error. But it might also be claimed that, if Marx's account of ideology is true, then all sets of ideas *must* be mere expressions of class interests, and therefore that Marx's own ideas cannot be true, but only such an expression. So Marx is seen as sawing off the branch he is sitting on.

In reply, it can first be said that not all accounts of the origins of beliefs throw doubt on the credibility of those beliefs. Take, for example, the following statement of a hapless mayor of Lincoln: 'There is no housing shortage in Lincoln today – just a rumour that is put about by people who have nowhere to live' (quoted by Hodges in *Logic*, p. 16). The same fact that is cited as motivating the 'rumour', and therefore casting doubt upon it, actually proves its truth. The fact that the workers are exploited may explain their belief that they are exploited – and also makes it true. Attempts to debunk views by 'chip-on-the-shoulder' explanations often ends with support for the views in this way.

But in order to defend his views in this way, Marx must first recognize – as indeed he does – that you can ask two questions about an idea: how did it originate?; and why we should believe that it is true? Sometimes, the answers to the second question are so good that the first question ceases to matter much, as with the pure natural sciences. Sometimes the same story will be told under both headings, as with the examples I have just used. In these cases, a particular class may be in a better position to know the truth than another class. It is, I would argue, a view essential to Marxism that the proletarian is in a better position to understand the truth about capitalist society than the bourgeois is. For instance, the bourgeois will easily believe in the myth of individual independence, since he or she dominates the workers on whom he or she is dependent, and thinks of this domination as independence. One of those workers is less likely to be fooled.

Overall, Marx holds that, while people's ideas are often distorted by their class position, so that the falsity of prevalent ideas is no accident, it still makes sense to pursue objective truth. This is what science does. Marx never thought, as some sociologists of science do today, that science is just another ideology. And in the social sphere, it is easier for a class that has nothing to hide to arrive at true opinions – 'nothing to hide' both in the sense of not being an oppressor of other classes, and in the sense of not being in such a hopeless situation that it wants to conceal its true case from itself.

Morality and anti-moralism

The second paradox could be seen as a special instance of the first. Marx's theories about capitalism have the consequence that capitalism ought to be overthrown and replaced by socialism. Marx has strong views on what constitutes a life suitable to human beings, and condemns social arrangements that prevent people having such a life. He condemns the cruelty and hypocrisy by which the ruling class defends its rule, in no uncertain terms. In this sense, Marx is a moralist. Yet, just as he seems to throw doubt on his own theory by (apparently) debunking theory in general, so he raises questions about his own moralizing by a number of remarks that seem to call into question morality as such – for instance, 'Law, morality and religion are to [the proletarian] so many bourgeois prejudices, behind which lurk in ambush just as many bourgeois interests' ('The Communist Manifesto', *The Revolutions of 1848*, p. 78). Someone who knew Marx reported that he always laughed when anyone mentioned morality.

Was Marx in some sense an amoralist? If so, what do we make of his own moral opinions?

That there is a real problem here is shown by a piece of the correspondence between Engels and Paul and Laura Lafargue (Marx's son-in-law and daughter). Engels tells Paul Lafargue,

> Marx would protest against the economic 'political and social ideal' which you attribute to him. When one is a 'man of science' one does not have an ideal; one works out scientific results, and when one is a party man to boot, one fights to put them into practice. But when one has an ideal, one cannot be a man of science, for one starts out with preconceptions. (*Engels/Lafargue Correspondence*, p. 235)

This is a confusing remark. On the one hand, Engels is making the correct point that one should not let any preconceived ideals affect one's scientific conclusions. But he also assumes that those conclusions can be 'put into practice', which seems to mean that they are in some sense ideals. His point seems to be ambiguous between the positivist idea that scientific facts are one thing and practical conclusions another, and the one cannot be derived from the other; and on the other hand the idea that, while scientific work does not have practical premisses, it does have practical conclusions – a position which I think can be defended, but which means that the 'man of science', as such, may be committed to the practical conclusions; in other words, that being a scientist and being a party activist are not just accidentally related. And certainly, *Capital* does seem to have practical conclusions by virtue of its scientific account of capitalism, not just as an afterthought. Perhaps Engels's lack of clarity is excusable due to the unbearably hot summer and the absence of lager beer in Worthing, where he was on holiday. The letter concludes:

> Here we are dying of heat, but we are pretty well nonetheless. Everyone sends Laura and you a thousand greetings. Unfortunately our stock of Pilsener is running out and it takes two days to replace it from Brighton! We live in a state of complete barbarism here. (p. 235)

A rather more balanced account of Marx's conception of the relation between scientific and political work is given by Lafargue himself in his reminiscences of Marx:

While he was of the opinion that every science must be cultivated for its own sake and that when we undertake scientific research we should not trouble ourselves about the possible consequences, nevertheless, he held that the man of learning, if he does not wish to degrade himself, must never cease to participate in public affairs – must not be content to shut himself up in his study or his laboratory, like a maggot in a cheese, and to shun the life and the social and political struggles of his contemporaries.

'Science must not be a selfish pleasure. Those who are so lucky as to be able to devote themselves to scientific pursuits should be the first to put their knowledge at the service of mankind.' One of his favourite sayings was, 'Work for the world.' (*Selected Works in Two Volumes*, vol. 1, pp. 81–2)

Now to look at possible interpretations of Marx's own ambivalent remarks about morality.

There are two readings of Marx's attitude to morality which I think are non-starters, and two others which are not fully accurate, though they come closer to the truth. The first non-starter is what Popper calls 'moral historicism'. This is the view that certain outcomes to history are inevitable, and we ought to work for these because they are inevitable. I don't think Marx was a historicist in any sense of the word, but this is the least plausible. He knew perfectly well that the Earth would eventually become uninhabitable and collapse into the Sun, but he did not think we should work to bring this about. Even the idea of progress is held very lightly by Marx and Engels, as expressed in Engels's reference to 'the conviction that humanity, at least at the present, moves on the whole in a progressive direction' (*Selected Works in Two Volumes*, vol. 1, p. 441). Marx and Engels's reasons for working for socialism have nothing to do with any supposed inevitability.

The second non-starter is the idea that Marx was a cynical Machiavellian who may have had moral ideals about his ends, but was prepared to use any means – as expressed in Brecht's remark that one who works for communism has, of all virtues, only one: that he works for communism. I see no reason to attribute this to Marx. He was prepared – as all practical people must be – to use certain bad means to good ends, as we all do when we accept surgical operations or policing. But he did not ever contemplate the sort of sacrifice of

137

innocent lives to a good goal that was taken for granted by Stalin, or even Churchill and Truman. He condemned his opponents, not just for their goals, but for the savagery or dishonesty with which they pursued them.

The third reading of Marx's ethics, which this time has at least some relation to the truth, is that he was a relativist, believing in different moralities for different classes, 'bourgeois morality' and 'proletarian morality'. Aside from the fact that when he expresses scepticism about morality he does not make this distinction, I think Marx's whole temper of mind is non-relativist. He seeks objectivity in knowledge, and he does not make the sort of division between knowledge and morality that is customary in empiricist philosophy. *Capital* is not a book of description and explanation with some moral passages added, it is moral by virtue of being descriptive and explanatory. But there is an element of truth in the class relativist position which we will come to shortly.

Finally, of the inadequate readings of Marx there is the one that appeals most to me: that Marx was what in religious circles would be called an antinomian, that is, someone who thinks that the way to live a good life is not by trying to be moral but by something else of which good action would be a side effect. In religious contexts this 'something else' is such things as faith in God, or following the Tao – or in St Augustine, simply love: *dilige et quod vis fac*, love and do what you will. In Marx it would be politics, both the practice of socialist politics here and now, and the experience of living in a socialist society in the future. Once again, there is an element of truth here, in that Marx rejects what I have elsewhere called the moralistic paradigm of morality: the belief that we become good by striving to act according to the moral law. But there is a more obvious source of Marx's disdain for the *word* 'morality'.

This source is Hegel. I am one of those who read Marx, in general, as much less Hegelian than he is often thought to be. I think the one enduring influence of Hegel's philosophy on Marx's mature thought is in his attitude to morality. I say 'attitude', for Marx says little explicitly about it, and one has to read between the lines.

When Engels, in a work written after Marx's death, settles accounts with Feuerbach, he sees Feuerbach's moral ideas as his weakest point, and praises Hegel by comparison. Although Marx's Feuerbachian period is in most ways a passage from Hegel to historical materialism, in ethics his way of overcoming Feuerbach – that is, by looking at people's concrete historical situations rather than their human essence – is also a way back to Hegel.

Hegel distinguishes *Moralität* (usually translated as 'morality') from *Sittlichkeit* (usually translated as ethical life). Each of them has a place in Hegel's system, but *Sittlichkeit* is the fuller and more mature. *Moralität* is roughly what I have called elsewhere the moralistic paradigm of ethics, exemplified by Kant. It is the morality of duty for duty's sake, of 'autonomous ethics' with no roots in human desires or institutions, supposedly the same for everyone whoever they are, and taking absolute priority over other motives for action. Hegel contrasts this with *Sittlichkeit,* an ethic rooted in the institutions within which human life finds its fulfilment. For Hegel this means primarily the family, civil society and the state, but a richer (and more accessible) version of this ethic is advocated by the English Hegelian F.H. Bradley in the chapter of his *Ethical Studies* called 'My station and its duties'. According to this, one's duties stem from what one is in society. For instance, if a man is a husband, a father, a citizen, a carpenter, a trade unionist and a friend of X, Y and Z, then what it means for him to be a good man is to be a good husband, father, citizen, carpenter, trade unionist and friend. This ethic has three immediate advantages. (1) It shows how there can be real moral conflicts, conflicts between duties, which many moralists deny. They are the conflicts between the duties of one role and those of another. Marx himself was often torn between his duty to his family as a husband and father, and his duty as a world citizen to work for the liberation of the oppressed. (2) Unlike Kant's morality, it shows a connection between human duties and human fulfilment and, unlike some other Enlightenment moralists, this connection is not that duties are somehow a means to self-interested ends. For it is in one's life as a family member, worker, friend etc. that one finds fulfilment, and it is just these roles that come with duties attached. (3) It holds up the possibility that an ethic can be objective. If we ask, What is a good person? it is easy for someone to say, 'That depends on your subjective value judgements'; but there are objective criteria for a good husband (he does not terrorize his wife), a good carpenter (he or she does not make things that fall apart), a good friend (he or she helps you out in time of need) and so on.

I would suggest that Marx's ethic is a version of this *Sittlichkeit*, and that his sarcastic remarks about morality are directed to *Moralität*. I say a version of *Sittlichkeit*, but not just any version, otherwise he would be defending the duty of the managing director to maximize profits for his shareholders, of the police to break picket lines in strikes, and so on. Indeed, even apart from Marx's class politics, there are problems for Bradley about what to make of the duties of a good burglar (not to leave fingerprints, or not to rob the poor perhaps). Of course the burglar's duties as burglar may conflict with the burglar's duty as a citizen to keep the law, but then so sometimes will the duties of a father (not to shop his son for smoking cannabis for instance). Some criterion is needed to judge the roles themselves, before we can take seriously the duties that they generate, otherwise we would have no reply to the guards at Auschwitz who said that they were only obeying orders.

It could be argued that tacitly, yet quite clearly, Marx has such a criterion: does the role depend on exploitation, or, on the contrary, does it promote human liberation? The duty of the trade unionist not to cross the picket line is upheld, the duty of a policeman to club down a demonstrator is not. This is importantly different from the view attributed to Lenin with some plausibility, and, less accurately, to Trotsky, according to which conduciveness or otherwise to human liberation directly and uniquely generates duties. This is the attitude expressed by Brecht that 'he who works for communism has of all the virtues only one: that he works for communism'. The view that I am claiming is implicit in Marx is not this: rather, the duties come from the roles, some of which (for example many friendships) have nothing to do with either exploitation or liberation. The relation to liberation comes in as a second order principle, by which we reject certain roles and prioritize others.

This may not be the last word on ethics, but it is at least a good part of ethics, and far removed from the cynical *realpolitik* of which Marx is often accused. On the other hand, it can be seen how this view has something in common with antinomianism (the rejection of the moralistic paradigm of ethics, *Moralität*), and something in common with class relativism (the endorsement, on class grounds, of the duties generated by certain roles, and not others).

Another word is necessary, though, in the light of history since Marx's time. In Marx's lifetime, few atrocities were committed by the left. The Jacobin terror was within living memory, but that was overshadowed both by much greater counter-revolutionary terror (after the fall of the Paris Commune, for example), and by the routine legal terror whereby, at the time of the French Revolution, English law hanged hungry children for stealing food. Furthermore, throughout the nineteenth century, even oppressive regimes were becoming more civilized in some ways: for instance, the use of torture declined throughout the nineteenth century, only to be revived in the twentieth. The atrocities of Marx's time were mostly economic rather than political, like the export of grain from Ireland during the potato famine, which killed one-and-a-half million people. He did not think it necessary to promulgate an ethic of 'the just war' to govern the behaviour of class warriors.

The history of the twentieth century shows the need for such an ethic. While Stalin's atrocities can be explained as done in the cause, not of communism, but of state capitalist counter-revolution (most of the leaders of the Bolshevik revolution were executed by Stalin), there are also questions about earlier Bolshevik practice. Even under Lenin and Trotsky, the Cheka (secret police) were guilty of crimes, usually (but not always) against the intentions of the Bolshevik leaders. For instance, on the night that the Supreme Soviet abolished capital punishment, the Cheka had all their prisoners shot, before the new law came into effect. While the Bolshevik leaders were obviously not directly responsible for this, they bear the responsibility for setting up a secret police force with such powers.

In the light of this, the work of such Marxists as Norman Geras to incorporate just war theory into the politics of Marxism is to be welcomed, and is not against the spirit of Marx. Some modern moral philosophers have made the distinction between the ethics of goals and the ethics of 'side-constraints', that is, of constraints on the way we should pursue those goals. Marx says a lot about goals and little about side-constraints, due, I have suggested, to the view that it was no longer necessary to make these explicit. But his polemics against the methods of his opponents shows a hatred of lies and cruelty, and abstention from lies (where possible) and (in all cases) from cruelty are the side-constraints required to avoid the atrocities of twentieth-century politics.

In summary, Marx's work does not give us a complete moral philosophy, nor was it his intention to do so. Nevertheless, his attitudes to ethical questions are not inconsistent, and are rational and decent ones. He is neither an immoralist nor an amoralist, though he rejects a certain kind of moralism.

Making history and historical determinism

The third paradox is beset by some of the most enduring academic legends about Marx. It is the supposed conflict between his historical determinism and his call to action to change the world. It is asked: if socialism must come about anyway, why work for it?

First, let me dispel some of the legends. Marx did not personify history or regard it as a suprapersonal agent. He was scathing about those who did:

> History does *nothing*; it 'does *not* possess immense riches', it 'does *not* fight battles'. It is *men*, real, living men, who do all this, who possess things and fight battles. It is not 'history' which uses men as means of achieving – as if it were an individual person – *its* own ends. History is *nothing* but the activity of men in pursuit of their ends. (*The Holy Family*, quoted by Bottomore and Rubel in their *Karl Marx: Selected Writings in Sociology and Social Philosophy*, p. 78)

The legend of Marx and Engels as idol-worshippers of history is taken to a great, but not untypical, extreme by Lewis Feuer in his introduction to his collection of their works:

> Engels at the end of 1893 comforted himself with a myth: 'But history is the cruellest of all goddesses, and she drives her triumphal car over heaps of corpses, not only in war, but also in "peaceful" economic development.' One remembered the cities depopulated and the countries denuded, and wondered how Engels could still in masochist fashion worship 'the cruellest of all goddesses'. (Feuer, ed. *Marx and Engels: Basic Writings on Politics and Philosophy*, pp. 28–9)

It is inconceivable how anyone can read this passage of Engels's in this way. It is as if someone were to quote St John's words that 'the whole world lieth in the hands of the evil one', comment that he was 'comforting himself' with a myth, and conclude that he was a Satanist. Engels is clearly using the metaphor – for that is what it is, not a 'myth' – to indicate that history, under conditions of class oppression, is a cruel process, and that consequently we should abolish those conditions and begin a new kind of history in which people make their future peacefully by conscious, collective decisions.

Marx and Engels's theory of history is indeed, in the proper sense of the word, determinist. That is to say, they regarded it as a process governed by causal laws. But this does not imply that anything is inevitable. All sciences treat their subject matters as governed by causal laws, but none, with the possible exception of cosmology, talk of inevitable outcomes. It would be nice to conclude that historical events are as much caused and as little inevitable as outcomes in biology or meteorology.

However, that would not quite represent Marx accurately, for two reasons. One is that he does sometimes talk as if some event is inevitable. I suspect that this is no more than 'cheering on the troops'. Marx, like most Victorians, was an incurable optimist and, like Queen Victoria herself, was 'not interested in the possibility of defeat'. The other reason is more significant. It is that Marx did believe in certain developmental tendencies of social systems – for instance, that under capitalism industry tends to become more capital-intensive, capital tends to become more concentrated, and so on. He probably thought that some of these tendencies were what we should now call positive feedback mechanisms – and positive feedback mechanisms will eventually destroy any system. For instance, if one set up a thermostat as a positive feedback mechanism instead of a negative one as they normally are – that is, if whenever the house got too hot an extra heat source was turned on, the house would soon become uninhabitable. If there are such positive feedback mechanisms in capitalism, it must eventually collapse. I think it is quite possible that this is true with reference to the environmental crisis. Here, we do have a doctrine of inevitability.

Two points should be made about this inevitability, though. (1) What is inevitable is not socialism or communism, but the collapse of capitalism. Marx had said in 'The Communist Manifesto' (*The Revolutions of 1848*, p. 68) that class struggles had always either ended in 'a revolutionary reconstruction of society at large, or in the common ruin of the contending classes'. In a letter about the criticisms of Mikhailovsky (*Selected Correspondence*, p. 313) he rejects the idea of historical inevitability except within the context of a particular mode of production, and points out that the ancient Roman class struggle did not lead to a revolutionary reconstruction. In fact it ended in the fall of Rome. Later Marxists have taken up this theme: Kautsky saw the alternative to socialism as capitalism stagnating and rotting; Rosa Luxemburg posed the alternative 'socialism or barbarism' – that is to say that, when capitalism collapsed, whether this led to socialism or barbarism depended on how well the proletariat was organized and what people did.

(2) The other point about this inevitability is that it is what might be called an open-ended inevitability. It is not like the inevitability that water will boil if it is sufficiently heated; it is more like the sort of prediction that might be made on the basis of knowledge of the geography, drainage system and climate of an area that sooner or later it will be subject to serious flooding.

We have seen one way in which such inevitability is compatible with human agency in making history: it is up to us what we do when the crash comes. But more can be said. Even the processes that develop inevitably are processes involving human actions. These actions themselves may be explained by historical laws, but that does not make them superfluous to the process: there is no process except through them. Even, say, something like the concentration of capital can happen only if people perform acts of working, investing, undercutting competitors in the market, buying up other firms, and so on. The point is that we can predict, with some degree of certainty, that people will do this. But no one is saying that the predicted outcome will occur *whatever people do*. There is no mystery about the partial predictability of a history that is made up of the free actions of men and women. They make their own history, but not in conditions they have chosen:

Men make their own history, but they do not make it just as they please; they do not make it under circumstances chosen by themselves, but under circumstances directly found, given and transmitted from the past. (*Selected Works in Two Volumes*, vol. 2, p. 315)

In the social production of their life, men enter into definite relations that are indispensable and independent of their will. (*Selected Works in One Volume*, p. 182)

The worker must work, the capitalist accumulate capital, the consumer consume, if they are to continue to exist – and so long as they do so, capitalism will be reproduced. We cannot change the course of history by altering the activities through which we make history, the activities of working and exchanging goods and marrying and raising children and talking to our friends. We can change it only by acting together in large numbers to change social structures.

So Marx does not make human action redundant, since for him history consists entirely of intentional human actions and their (often unintended) effects; moreover, certain outcomes are open, and what happens depends on how large numbers of people decide to act. Yet these successions of human actions are governed by laws of tendency, generated by the structures in which human beings find themselves, which are, for each generation, independent of their will.

Marx Today

Marxism after Marx

The influence of Marx throughout the late-nineteenth and twentieth centuries was immense, and it is not yet exhausted. But, as with any thinker who has changed the course of history, the effects of his work have not always been what he would have predicted or wanted. At the extreme: for over twenty years, world Marxism was dominated by Stalin, whose policies had as little in common with Marx's as the tortures of the Inquisition had with the teachings of Jesus. This book would be incomplete without some sort of assessment of Marx's successors, particularly as he is habitually judged by their achievements or crimes. After this, it will be useful to relate his ideas to the world that is emerging in the twenty-first century.

From 1917 onwards, the socialist movements originating from Marx have been divided into two hostile camps: social democrats and communists. Before 1917, the terms 'social democrat' and 'communist' were more or less synonymous, and most people who were called either were Marxists. All shared both commitment to democracy and the aim of transferring productive resources to common ownership. If one reads the Marxists of the 1880s, 1890s and 1900s, revolutionary aims co-exist with parliamentary work, and parties tend to have maximum and minimum programmes, the latter to be worked for now, the former in the event of a revolution – indeed there is quite a lot to be said for this position – though there were always a few ultra-lefts who rejected parliament outright, like William Morris in England and the 'otzovists' in Russia. After the Russian Revolution, workers' movements everywhere split into those that took it as their model, appropriating the label 'communists', and those that did not, and envisaged a parliamentary road to socialism, appropriating the label 'social democrats'. At first, the differences were not as great as they were later to become. Both believed in some sort of democracy, the communists claiming – not without reason – that the 'soviets' or workers' councils in Russia were a fuller sort of democracy than parliament. Social democrats still aimed at fully fledged socialism, as 'Clause 4' of the 1918 Constitution of the British Labour Party illustrates, with an admirable clarity not copied by more recent political statements. By stages, the power in Russia passed from the elected soviets to the party bureaucracy, and 'elections' for the soviets became a one-party matter; and Western social democratic parties back-pedalled on their socialist aims till they became, also by stages, the mildly interventionist liberal parties that they are today. Clearly, neither the Chinese Communist Party nor the British Labour Party nor the SPD has much in common with Marx, as I write in the early twenty-first century.

But how do these tendencies relate to Marxism? On the subject of different types of democracy, as we have seen, there is some ambiguity in Marx himself. He holds up the Paris Commune of 1871 as a new, higher type of democracy, and Lenin takes this as his starting point in *The State and Revolution*. But Marx also held out the possibility that in the most advanced parliamentary countries (which even though they did not have universal suffrage were clearly moving in that direction) socialist revolution might come legally, through the election of a workers' party, to a parliamentary majority. Legally, but not necessarily peacefully, since a capitalist rebellion against the workers' government might occur. Also, it can be argued that, while universal suffrage is now widespread, it has been accompanied by a shift in power from the elected to the unelected parts of the state, which make the prospects for the UK and USA more akin to those of Germany under Bismarck than to those of the UK under Gladstone or the USA under Lincoln.

The communists in 1917 were close to the Marx of *The Civil War in France* in their belief that the apparatus of the capitalist state could not be taken over but had to be 'smashed'. And the experience of history has confirmed this belief: wherever governments committed to socialism have been elected to power, the forces of the old state apparatus (notably the standing army) have always been strong enough either to deflect them from their socialist purpose or to overthrow them. The typical case is Chile, where Allende's elected socialist coalition was overthrown by the army under General Pinochet, with US support, and replaced by a regime of blood and torture, to the admiration of British Conservatives. I do not think that anyone who studies the statements of politicians of all parties can doubt that a similar coup would be attempted if a seriously socialist government were elected in the United Kingdom.

Hence, at a theoretical level, communists can claim that all the evidence supports their claims about what is and is not possible – I mean communists of the 1917 type, for many of what used to be the communist parties are now effectively social democrats. On the other hand, practically, the record of communists in power is everywhere one of eventually destroying democracy where it had existed, either in its soviet or its parliamentary guise. While some communist countries have had a better record of economic and social policy than is commonly admitted in the West, none has established popular control either of the state or the economy – hence none can be called socialist in the sense that Marx understood the word. Social democratic governments on the other hand, while also abandoning the goal of popular control of the economy, have presided over the development of what are probably the best societies to live in in modern times, if not ever, upon the basis of strong trade unions and co-operative movements, redistributive taxation, a welfare state and a mixed economy. Whether this social democratic option is still on the menu since globalization is a moot point.

Marxist parties do exist that are committed to government of state and economy by elected workers' councils on the model of the soviets during and immediately after the Russian Revolution, while they were still democratic institutions in which communists competed for election with social democrats, anarchists and even liberals.

There are two traditions of such parties: Trotskyists and council communists, differing over the role of the party (essential for Trotskyists, dispensable for council communists) and their analysis of the states governed by communists (deformed workers' states according to the Trotskyists, state capitalist according to the council communists). The Socialist Workers' Party in the UK, and its sister parties elsewhere, hold an intermediate position, agreeing with the Trotskyists about the party and with the council communists about state capitalism. This is perhaps the 'pure Marxist' position, though, given Marx's aversion to sectarian policies and his preference for broad workers' movements, even if they are astray on theory, I cannot see him fitting easily into these groups.

Marx's theories and recent developments

We have seen that Marx's 'predictions' are not prophecies, but are the identification of tendencies always inherent in capitalism, which develop as it progresses, and will continue to develop short of either revolution or catastrophic collapse. His mistake regarding these tendencies was usually 'telescoping', that is, exaggerating the speed at which they would develop. As to the tendencies themselves, he was amazingly accurate. This can be seen in several instances.

Globalization

As we have seen, Marx mistakenly thought that the nation state was already on its way out, even within capitalism, in his own time. But, though this was a premature obituary in the mid-nineteenth century, something of the sort is happening today. The coming of supra-national institutions to Europe, which Marx thought was imminent, has at last happened. But more importantly, the global market has everywhere undermined the economic sovereignty of nations. National governments can no longer protect the interests of their own people against global market forces. There are those who welcome this development and those who resist it. Marx would not belong unambiguously to either camp. His 1847 speech on free trade recognizes the adverse effects that free trade has on the workers, yet concludes by supporting free trade as it will make economic contradictions act on a larger scale, leading to the emancipation of the proletariat. Marx was an inveterate optimist, and could not believe that things would go on getting worse. One could argue today that our task for the foreseeable future is not to make the world a better place, but only to slow the pace at which it gets worse, but Marx could not have thought like that. He clearly thought that globalization is not only inevitable, but potentially (and in the long term actually) beneficial in uniting humankind into one economic community. Yet he could not have welcomed the erosion of even such economic democracy as existed under capitalism, which was itself the achievement of over a century of workers' struggles. He would have seen a solution, not in a reversion to national sovereignty, but in the establishment of international democratic institutions on a world scale, starting no doubt from some sort of international workers' association such as he tried to build in his own lifetime, and successive generations of Marxists have tried to build since. But eventually the solution would have to be some kind of world federation in a socialist context – a planetary democracy with economic as well as political power, no doubt with many powers decentralized, but with no private institution with the wealth and power to overawe elected ones.

It is often assumed, particularly in the wake of the fall of 'state socialism' in Eastern Europe, that the demands for democracy and for the free market go together. Yet the free market means that, within corporations, power is wielded by people unelected by those whom the power affects; and in the relations between corporations, power is at the mercy of impersonal, 'alienated' economic forces. Neither sort of power is compatible with democracy. What can be learnt from Marx here is that in the modern world the real alignment of forces is 'the market versus democracy', that democracy can only win if it becomes global, and that this cannot be done by rationalizing capitalism, but only by abolishing it.

Proletarianization

In Marx's time the proletariat was a minority everywhere except in Britain, but it was a growing minority, and Marx assumes throughout his work that it was 'the coming class'. Today, this is widely held to be outdated. In the most advanced societies, particularly the

151

English-speaking ones, the proletariat is declining in numbers, and some would say is a minority. (It should be recognized that orthodox sociologists' definitions of class are different from Marx's that depend on relation to the means of labour, not on education or lifestyle. Probably on Marx's definitions the proletariat in the UK is between two-thirds and three-quarters of the population.) But on a world scale, the proletariat is still growing. It is very close to being the majority class of humankind. Its decline in some rich countries is parasitic upon this fact, just as there have always been suburbs of capitalist cities where the proletariat is absent.

From Marx's point of view, the growth in the world proletariat is important because the possibility of emancipation for humankind as a whole is bound up with the proletariat. This is not because of any kind of mystical 'proletarian messianism' as is often alleged, but because alone among oppressed classes its conditions of life make it possible for it to unite, to organize democratically, to resist collectively and, under favourable circumstances, to take over the production process. If the proletariat were really no longer 'the coming class' but a passing class, the possibility of any democratic reconstruction of society would be passing too, on Marx's assumptions.

In the 1960s there were controversies between those Marxists who held to the idea of the unique emancipatory potential of the proletariat, and 'Third-Worldists' who turned instead to the peasant classes of the poorer countries. Today, there can be no such controversy. To look to the proletariat for emancipation is for the most part to look to the newly industrialized countries of the 'Third World'.

Concentration of capital

Competition has never had all the virtues that Adam Smith claimed for it, but it did have some virtues. In early capitalism, no single firm was big enough by itself to appreciably alter the state of the market, or to bring pressure to bear on political authorities. Marx always argued that, as capitalism developed, ownership of capital would become more and more concentrated, tending towards monopoly, until not only the interest of the proletariat, but even the 'public interest' within a bourgeois parliamentary state would constrain the government to take over or control great corporations. Yet within Marx's lifetime, there was nothing like the great multinational corporations of today, many of which have turnovers greater than the national income of many medium-sized countries.

Marx was something of an optimist about human rationality, and would probably not have believed that elected governments would ever permit such large concentrations of irresponsible power, just as Engels believed that European nations would never again go to war, given the destructive potential of weapons by the end of his life.

Be that as it may, concentration of capital has certainly grown apace in the hundred-and-twenty years since Marx's death, and the case for public ownership and democratic control has become overwhelming for anyone who values democracy at all.

Increasing inequality

The mature Marx did not believe that workers would always get worse and worse off under capitalism. He defended the value both of labour legislation (such as the Ten Hours Act of 1846), and of trade unions, as means by which the lot of workers could be improved under capitalism. But he does seem to have held that inequalities of wealth would increase. Yet from the late-nineteenth till the late-twentieth century, inequalities within developed countries became less marked, precisely because of such trade-union actions and interventions by democratic parliaments as Marx defended – though in Britain, since Thatcher, this trend has been reversed.

However, the global picture is not so rosy. Rich countries get richer and poor countries get, at least relatively (often absolutely) poorer. It becomes clear that inequality of wealth is not a survival from pre-capitalist times, but a developing tendency of capitalism. Of course, there are those who claim that some inequalities are just, as based on different abilities, but no one in their right mind could claim this of the inequalities that exist between rich and poor countries today.

The question is often posed whether Marx's ideas are 'out of date'. If all that is meant is 'out of fashion', we should not pay this question any mind. The question about ideas is whether they are true or false, not whether they are fashionable or unfashionable. Indeed, Marxism has gone in and out of fashion several times since Marx's death, and no doubt will continue to do so. But there are two ways in which Marx's ideas could have become dated, rather than merely unfashionable. Firstly, Marx claimed to have inaugurated a science, and while non-scientific ideas do not progress and therefore do not go out of date, scientific ideas do both of these things. If there had been real progress in social science since Marx's time, his theories might have been left behind like Newton's theories were with the discoveries of Einstein. Some think this has happened, but certainly, so far as sociology is concerned, no new theory has won a general consensus, and it is arguable that those social scientists studying societies using Marxist theoretical tools are still producing the best work in this area. In economics the situation is rather different; Marx is widely regarded as 'old hat', but the current theories are not so much refutations of Marxism as they are theories about different things; and once again, none of these theories commands a consensus; the dominance of some over others is probably explained by political rather than scientific considerations. So the claim that Marx is out of date because he has been superseded by superior social scientific theories is, to say the least, unproven and contentious.

But there is, secondly, another way in which Marx's ideas could have become out of date. Many of them (not quite all) are about a specific period of history, namely capitalism, and more particularly, a capitalism that had outlived its progressive phase. Marx himself would have been very pleased if his ideas had become out of date in one way, namely by the replacement of capitalism with socialism. So it is legitimate to ask whether changes in the world since Marx's time have rendered his ideas irrelevant.

The main reason why Marx's ideas are treated as out of date in recent times – that is, since about 1990 – is that the regimes in Eastern Europe calling themselves Marxist have collapsed. It has always struck me as odd that this event has been seen in the West as a reason for rejecting Marxism. After all, everyone knew, while those regimes still existed, that they were not good examples of socialism as understood by Marx, and indeed Western Marxists spent a huge proportion of their time and energy analysing exactly what was wrong with them – were they 'state capitalist', or a new form of exploitation called 'bureaucratic collectivism', or degenerated workers' states that needed political revolutions to set them on a socialist course (Trotsky's position), or a kind of socialism that had been deformed by survivals of the autocratic past of most of those countries, or what? That they lacked political and industrial democracy, and some of the civil liberties that go with democracy, was well known. Nothing new and bad was discovered about them when the regimes fell; it was all stale news. One might have expected a *revival* of Marxism since it was no longer discredited by association with these regimes, and in the long term, that may yet happen. But at the time, many erstwhile Marxists suddenly came to see Marxism as 'out of date'. I have elsewhere compared this loss of nerve with a historical parallel: in 1789, all good people were delighted at the beginning of the French Revolution. Later, some turned against it because of the Jacobin terror, some because of the corruption of the Directory, some because of the militarism of Napoleon. All these are honourable reasons for doing so. But anyone who turned against it because Napoleon lost the Battle of Waterloo could only be described as a coward and a turncoat. Those who abandoned Marxism in 1990 are in the same category.

But what of the claim that since the whole world is now (very nearly) one capitalist market, history has come to an end, and future developments can only be within capitalism? Aside from the fact that the global market now has an odds-on chance of ending history in a more radical way – by an ecological disaster destroying life on Earth – sometime in the next hundred years, there is another way of looking at the apparent global victory of capitalism.

Let us start by looking at Marx's own view of the prospects for socialism. We have seen that at some points during the mid-nineteenth century revolutions, Marx thought for a while that an early proletarian revolution was on the cards. Later, he realized that it had not been, that the world had not yet been ripe for socialism. However, he certainly assumed towards the end of his life that it soon would be. But we have also seen Marx's tendency to 'telescope' future developments, to see as imminent what was indeed coming, but slowly. Almost certainly, a proletarian revolution could not have happened during the nineteenth century. Indeed, when the Russian

Revolution did occur in 1917, many Marxists, including Plekhanov, the founder of Russian Marxism and no mean thinker, thought it premature. In a sense, Trotsky and (sometimes) Lenin agreed with them, thinking that a revolution in the industrialized West was necessary if the Russian Revolution was to succeed. But the Western nations were too busy exploiting the colonized countries to make their own revolutions. And during the Cold War period, the Cold War itself precluded revolutions, since all radical opposition was tarred with the brush of the Cold War enemy.

But in the twenty-first century, the global market that Marx predicted has arrived, the old colonized countries have won political independence, and the world proletariat bids fair to become the majority of humankind. Perhaps the conditions for workers' power envisaged by Marx, so far from being dated to the nineteenth century, have only just been realized in the twenty-first.

Of course, despite their political independence, the 'Third World' countries are still being exploited through investment, debt and unfair trade. That makes workers' power in the rich countries an unlikely prospect. But in the newly industrialized countries, it has become a possibility for the first time. Against it, there is the military power of the rich countries which, as the Iraq War has shown, can be used to remove a government that the rich countries do not like. But it is hard to believe that this could be done if the country or countries concerned had a population of over one hundred million and were overwhelmingly behind their socialist government. After all, the USA was beaten in Vietnam, though by a peasant rather than a proletarian movement. And the governments that attacked Iraq no doubt had the bully's instinct for hitting only smaller boys. If we were to see a socialist India, Indonesia or Brazil, the flame might well spread, and the exploiting countries might be unable to stop it.

To sum up: what aspects of the modern world can Marx still draw our attention to and help us to understand, and not to underestimate? Why should we revisit Marx after over a hundred years of history? There are five issues that I would like to mention here.

Firstly, most obviously, the centre of Marx's view of society is the concept of class. Class exploitation is the invisible form of oppression today. I recently saw a Liberal Democrat member of parliament on the

TV, saying, truly enough, that parliament was dominated by white middle-class males, and going on to say that we needed more women, ethnic minorities and disabled people in parliament. Despite characterizing the existing parliament as middle class, she did not say that we needed more working-class MPs. Of course, this could have been a slip in a hurried response, but it is fairly typical, not only of liberals but of socialists too. Class is the one form of oppression that they do not notice, despite the fact that the working class is larger and more oppressed than any other oppressed group, and that, whereas something has been achieved by all other oppressed groups in the last fifty years, the working class, in the UK at least, is more oppressed – and less represented in parliament – than it was fifty years ago. Even if Marx is wrong in holding that class exploitation is the cause of other forms of exploitation (I happen to think that he was right about this), the reminder that such exploitation exists is valuable and timely.

Secondly, for Marx, great inequalities of wealth are the result of exploitation. Everyone today is aware of the division of the world into rich and poor countries. But the terms 'rich' and 'poor', while descriptively accurate, disguise the fact that the rich can only be rich because they exploit the poor, and indeed that, since money is essentially nothing but a token of power over the labour of others, great inequality is not only caused by but *essentially consists in* the oppression of the poor by the rich. This was not discovered by Marx: several of the Fathers of the Church were quite explicit that you could not be rich except by robbing the poor, so that setting up a flow of wealth the other way was not 'charity' but the repayment of what had been wrongfully appropriated. But Marx was the first to show the mechanism by which this exploitation takes place under market conditions.

So the division into rich and poor nations is not a brute fact, but something given by destiny. We laugh at the Victorians for singing,

> The rich man in his castle,
> The poor man at his gate,
> God made them high and lowly
> And ordered their estate.

But most people's only difference from this view today is that they attribute the division to luck rather than to God. Marx shows that the division into rich and poor is made not by either God or luck, but by robbery.

Both the invisibility of class exploitation and complacency about the rich–poor divide between countries may stem from the fact that, in capitalist societies, people think oppression means what it meant in pre-capitalist societies, that is, personal relations of mastery and servitude; where this does not exist, people do not believe that there can be oppression. But in capitalist societies, such personal relations are not the main form that oppression takes. Marx has shown that inequality in ownership of the sort of things that everyone depends on is the basis of all oppression. The worker who has a job also has 'master–slave' relations with his or her boss. But the unemployed worker, who has not, is the more oppressed.

This is why it is never possible to 'level up'. All could not have servants, because no one would then be the servant; all could not be capital owners, because capital is useless without propertiless workers to employ; indeed, all could not be car owners, because the planet could not sustain the pollution that this would cause. Ownership of what others lack is both what enables the owner to benefit at the expense of the non-owner, and is also what deprives the non-owner of basic freedoms: if someone blocks my access to light, it is as if they blinded me; if they block my access to the means of labour, it is as if they cut off my hands; yet what is property, if not the power to block other people's access to something? The illusion that keeps people's consciences clear in capitalist society is the illusion that property is a relation between the owner and the owned, and does not affect anyone else. Marx shows that one can oppress people without ever bossing them around or having a 'master–slave' relationship with them. You can be an oppressor simply by owning what other people need and lack. For there are kinds of property (for instance, capital) that have value only if others need and lack them; and this need and lack constitutes oppression.

Thirdly, the division into rich and poor countries is one of the two greatest problems confronting humankind today. The environmental crisis is the other. It is often alleged that Marx has nothing to say about this, apart from a few remarks like those mentioned on pp. 30–1 on the duty of humankind to care for the earth, and the critique of environmentally short-sighted methods in agriculture (see John Bellamy Foster, 2002). However, the distinction between exchange-value-driven and use-value-driven production may be exactly the distinction needed for an ecological economics. Exchange-value-driven production (production for profitable sale) systematically ignores all effects of the production process apart from financial cost and return, hence it ignores all environmental effects, as well as effects on the workers' health and happiness. Use-value-driven production takes into account any use-value that the production process either creates or destroys. These will include environmental and human effects as well as 'products'. This means that economic decision-making under socialism (which Marx conceives as a use-value-driven mode of production) would be very different from under capitalism. All foreseeable effects, good and bad, of any decision would have to be taken into account. But this would mean deciding between *incommensurable* values of various effects. Hence, as I have said in chapter five, mathematical calculation would not be the basis of decision-making. You cannot subtract three oranges from five apples.

It seems to me that, for these reasons and some to be dealt with under point four, environmentally sound economics would have to be socialist economics, and would involve developing rational ways of decision-making which are not calculative. This should not be impossible, since non-economic decision-making is non-calculative already.

The fourth question is about the attitude we should take to technology. Here, I think Marx has two lessons to teach – which on the surface may seem to pull in opposite directions, but which are both required for a balanced approach to the place of technology in modern life.

On the one hand, Marx sees technology as the foundation of human liberation. As we have seen, he thinks that slavery could not have been abolished without the steam engine and the spinning jenny; in general, human liberation from human oppressors presupposes the liberation of humankind at large from overwork. Only when it is possible for all to have enough leisure and culture to participate in the management of society, is democracy possible in the state or in industry. The reduction of the working day is the foundation of all culture and freedom, and only by technology can the working day be reduced for all. Marx is aware that with technical progress new needs are created, but thinks that, even so, labour can really be lightened by labour-saving technology.

But as we have also seen, Marx was well aware that the technical progress that was taking place so rapidly in his early lifetime had not lightened labour for the proletarians. It had the potential for doing so, but under capitalist conditions it had been used at first to lengthen the working day. (Such paradoxes still happen today, at a more advanced technological level. E-mail enables you to write a letter in two minutes instead of ten, but as a result, where you used to spend the first twenty minutes of the day answering letters, you now spend the first two hours deleting e-mails.) But Marx's point is, of course, that the capitalist use of technology militates against its tendency to save labour.

But the capitalist use of technology does more than this. Many people have noticed the runaway, out-of-control nature of modern technology. For Marx, this is an example of the out-of-control nature of capitalist markets in general. The laws of the markets make certain outcomes happen even if no one desires them, and there is no procedure available to prevent those unwanted outcomes. This is what I have called the 'sorcerer's apprentice' aspect of capitalism: technology increases human powers, but market forces prevent human beings from having power over those powers. This is a feature of uncontrolled markets, even without high technology. However, out-of-controlness does not matter so much when the powers that are out of control are very limited in effect. If you are careering downhill with faulty brakes, you are a much greater danger to yourself and others if you are in a lorry than if you are on a bike. If you are chopping down a rainforest, you cannot do as much harm with an axe as with mechanical means of deforestation. The development of high technology within capitalism means that out-of-control powers have greater and greater effects.

I think this is the truth in Marx's claim that, just as feudalism could not use steam-mill technology and so had to give way to capitalism, capitalism in turn cannot cope with technology beyond a certain level, and must give way to socialism. As with all parallels between the feudalism–capitalism transition and the capitalism–socialism transition, there are asymmetries. Feudalism just could not produce steam mills; they could not have fitted into its relations of production. Capitalism can produce high technology – very likely there is no ceiling on what it can produce. But it cannot stop that technology from having catastrophic effects on life on Earth. Climate change is a case in point. It is very difficult, if not impossible, for governments of capitalist societies to sufficiently regulate the amount of pollution that causes this – or indeed, to force powerful rogue states like the USA to conform even to such limits as are agreed.

And finally, the fifth point, in comparison with the issues of world poverty and the environmental crisis, the question of the survival or demise of democracy may seem small fry. Nevertheless there are (or were) considerable advantages to living in a democracy. Although it has never been possible in any democracy to elect just any government that the people want, it has been possible to oust a particularly unpopular government without bloodshed. Democracies usually have more personal liberties than undemocratic states, though there are anomalies: for instance, some of the undemocratic communist regimes of Eastern Europe in the 1970s and 1980s had more personal liberties in sexual matters than the highly democratic Irish Republic. But democracies do not usually use torture at home, though those with 'interests' abroad often do there. The same goes for capital punishment, if one excepts the USA (whose claim to be a democracy is anyway contentious, due to the difficulties of registering to vote). And democracy was in the twentieth century a mechanism whereby some of the most powerful institutions of society could be brought to defend some of the weakest members of society.

But in recent years, two tendencies can be noted in all parliamentary democracies: political power has shifted from the legislature – usually the only elected part of the state apparatus – to the executive, bureaucratic and military parts of the state, which are unelected; and economic power now eludes the state as a whole, and has shifted to multinational corporations. Marx more than anyone has pointed out both that political power has economic foundations, and that the state is not just the legislature but the coercive and administrative machinery. If the elected part of the state had considerable political and economic power in some countries for a while in the twentieth century, that power itself had a foundation at the point of production in the powerful democratic organizations of the working class, the trade unions. With the decline of trade-union power it is no surprise that democracy has increasingly become a facade, like the survival of the republican institutions of ancient Rome into the age of the emperors. Increasingly, we need to learn from Marx that if we are serious about democracy we must have a democratic army (that is, a citizens' militia) and democratic economic corporations (that is, socialism) as well as a democratic legislature. Otherwise we will eventually lose all the advantages that democracy brought.

To refer back to the quotation with which I opened this book: the message of Marx is that if humankind is to be free in the twenty-first century – and perhaps even if it is to survive into the twenty-second – we need common ownership and democratic control of the productive resources of the planet.

Bibliography

Suggestions for further reading

For detailed biographical information, David McLellan's *Karl Marx* is essential, with Francis Wheen's book *Karl Marx: a Life* supplementing it in a lively way.

In reading Marx's own writings, it is best to start with *The Communist Manifesto* as the most comprehensive short account of Marx's mature political standpoint. If using the Pelican Marx Library editions it can be found in *The Revolutions of 1848*. It should be remembered that it *is* a manifesto, and therefore includes quite a few 'conclusions without premisses'. For Marx's politics the other most useful volume in that edition is *The First International and After*, which includes his address on the Paris Commune and his 'Critique of the Gotha Programme'.

For Marx's theory of history and society, *The German Ideology* part 1 is essential. C.J. Arthur's edition is good and accessible, and includes some useful supplementary material. On Marx's economic thought, *Value, Price and Profit*, also called *Wages, Price and Profit*, is the easiest thing to read. Eventually, any serious student of Marx must read volume 1 of *Capital*, but unless you are confident with abstract arguments, it may be best to skip the first nine chapters on first reading. The historical part of *Capital* is readable in style, though disturbing in content.

Marx's early thought can also be difficult, though the sections on alienation and humanism are heady stuff. All the important works written before 1845 are available in the Pelican volume *Early Writings*. I recommend William Morris's fantasy novel *News from Nowhere*, set in a future communist England, as throwing light on the ideals of the young Marx in particular, though one should bear in mind Marx's criticism of utopias, and William Morris's feeling for pre-capitalist societies, which was not shared by Marx.

Books referred to in the text

Althusser, Louis, *For Marx*. Penguin, Harmondsworth, 1969.

Benner, Erica, *Really Existing Nationalisms*. Oxford University Press, Oxford, 1995.

Bottomore, T.B. and Rubel, M., *Karl Marx: Selected Writings in Sociology and Social Philosophy*. Penguin, Harmondsworth, 1963.

Bradley, F.H., *Ethical Studies*. Oxford University Press, Oxford, 1962.

Callinicos, Alex, *The Revolutionary Ideas of Karl Marx*. Bookmarks, London, 1983.

Carver, Terrell, *Friedrich Engels*. Macmillan, Basingstoke, 1989.

—— *The Postmodern Marx*. Manchester University Press, Manchester, 1998.

Cohen, G.A., *Marx's Theory of History: a Defence*. Oxford University Press, Oxford, 1978.

Collier, Andrew, *Socialist Reasoning*. Pluto Press, London and Barnes and Noble, Savage, Maryland, 1990.

Engels, Frederick, *The Peasant War in Germany*. Lawrence and Wishart, London, 1956.

—— *Anti-Dühring*. Progress Publishers, Moscow, 1969.

—— *Correspondence with Paul and Laura Lafargue*. Foreign Languages Publishing House, Moscow, 1959.

Feuer, Lewis, *Marx and Engels: Basic Writings on Politics and Philosophy*. Collins, 1969.

Foster, John Bellamy, 'Marx's ecology in historical perspective' in *International Socialism*, no. 96, Autumn 2002.

Geras, Norman, *Marx and Human Nature: Refutation of a Legend*. Verso, London, 1983.

Hodges, Wilfrid, *Logic*. Penguin, Harmondsworth, 1977.

Honderich, Ted, 'Against Teleological Historical Materialism', in *Inquiry*, 25, 1982.

Lafargue, Paul, 'Reminiscences of Marx' in Karl Marx, *Selected Works in Two Volumes*.

—— *The Right to be Lazy*. Charles H. Kerr, Chicago, 1989. (See also 'Engels'.)

Lenin, Vladimir, *Selected Works*. Lawrence and Wishart, London, 1968.

Liebknecht, Wilhelm, 'Reminiscences of Marx' in Karl Marx, *Selected Works in Two Volumes*.

McLellan, David, *Karl Marx: His Life and Thought*. Macmillan, London and Basingstoke, 1973.

Marx, Karl, *Selected Works in Two Volumes*. Lawrence and Wishart, London, 1942.

—— *Capital, Volume One* (trans. Moore and Aveling) Lawrence and Wishart, London, 1959.

—— *Early Writings*. Penguin, Harmondsworth, 1975.

—— *The Revolutions of 1848*. Penguin, Harmondsworth, 1973.

—— *Surveys from Exile*. Penguin, Harmondsworth, 1973.

—— *Grundrisse*. Penguin, Harmondsworth, 1973.

—— *The First International and After*. Penguin, Harmondsworth, 1974.

—— *Capital, Volume One* (trans. Ben Fowkes) Penguin, Harmondsworth, 1976.

—— *Capital, Volume Three*. Penguin, Harmondsworth, 1981.

Marx, Karl and Engels, Frederick, *Selected Works in One Volume*, Lawrence and Wishart, London, 1968.

—— *The German Ideology*, ed. R. Pascal, International Publishers, New York, 1947.

—— *Selected Correspondence*. Progress Publishers, Moscow, 1965.

—— *The German Ideology, Part one* (ed. C.J. Arthur), Lawrence and Wishart, London, 1970.

—— *Collected Works*, volume 5, Lawrence and Wishart, London, 1976.

Mehring, Franz, *Karl Marx*. Allen and Unwin, London, 1936.

Morris, William, 'News from Nowhere' in *Selected Writings*, Nonesuch, London, 1948.

Plekhanov, Georgi, *Selected Philosophical Works*, volume 3, Progress Publishers, Moscow, 1976.

Tawney, R.H., *Religion and the Rise of Capitalism*. Penguin, Harmondsworth, 1938.

Thomson, George, *The First Philosophers*. Lawrence and Wishart, London, 1972.

Weber, Max, *The Protestant Ethic and the Spirit of Capitalism.* Allen and
Unwin, London, 1930.

Wheen, Francis, *Karl Marx: a Life.* W.W. Norton & Company, 2000.

Index